METHAMPHETAMINE

by Hal Marcovitz

DRUG
EDUCATION
LIBRARY

LUCENT BOOKS

An imprint of Thomson Gale, a part of The Thomson Corporation

THOMSON
™
GALE

Detroit • New York • San Francisco • San Diego • New Haven, Conn.
Waterville, Maine • London • Munich

THOMSON

™

GALE

© 2006 Thomson Gale, a part of The Thomson Corporation.

Thomson and Star Logo are trademarks and Gale and Lucent Books are registered trademarks used herein under license.

For more information, contact
Lucent Books
27500 Drake Rd.
Farmington Hills, MI 48331-3535
Or you can visit our Internet site at http://www.gale.com

LIBRARY OF CONGRESS CATALOGING-IN-PUBLICATION DATA

Marcovitz, Hal.
  Methamphetamine / by Hal Marcovitz.
    p. cm. — (Drug education library)
  Inculdes bibliographical references and index.
  ISBN 1-59018-418-1 (hardcover : alk. paper)
  1. Methamphetamine abuse—Juvenile literature. I. Title. II. Series.
  RC568.A45M37 2005
  362.29'9—dc22

                                                                2005018294

Printed in the United States of America

Contents

Foreword

The development of drugs and drug use in America is a cultural paradox. On the one hand, strong, potentially dangerous drugs provide people with relief from numerous physical and psychological ailments. Sedatives like Valium counter the effects of anxiety; steroids treat severe burns, anemia, and some forms of cancer; morphine provides quick pain relief. On the other hand, many drugs (sedatives, steroids, and morphine among them) are consistently misused or abused. Millions of Americans struggle each year with drug addictions that overpower their ability to think and act rationally. Researchers often link drug abuse to criminal activity, traffic accidents, domestic violence, and suicide.

These harmful effects seem obvious today. Newspaper articles, medical papers, and scientific studies have highlighted the myriad problems drugs and drug use can cause. Yet, there was a time when many of the drugs now known to be harmful were actually believed to be beneficial. Cocaine, for example, was once hailed as a great cure, used to treat everything from nausea and weakness to colds and asthma. Developed in Europe during the 1880s, cocaine spread quickly to the United States where manufacturers made it the primary ingredient in such everyday substances as cough medicines, lozenges, and tonics. Likewise, heroin, an opium derivative, became a popular painkiller during the late nineteenth century. Doctors and patients flocked to American drugstores to buy heroin, described as the optimal cure for even the worst coughs and chest pains.

As more people began using these drugs, though, doctors, legislators, and the public at large began to realize that they were more damaging than beneficial. After years of using heroin as a painkiller, for example, patients began asking their doctors for larger and stronger doses. Cocaine users reported dangerous side effects, including hallucinations and wild mood shifts. As a result, the U.S. government initiated more stringent regulation of many powerful and addictive drugs, and in some cases outlawed them entirely.

A drug's legal status is not always indicative of how dangerous it is, however. Some drugs known to have harmful effects can be purchased legally in the United States and elsewhere. Nicotine, a key ingredient in cigarettes, is known to be highly addictive. In an effort to meet their bodies' demands for nicotine, smokers expose themselves to lung cancer, emphysema, and other life-threatening conditions. Despite these risks, nicotine is legal almost everywhere.

Other drugs that cannot be purchased or sold legally are the subject of much debate regarding their effects on physical and mental health. Marijuana, sometimes described as a gateway drug that leads users to other drugs, cannot legally be used, grown, or sold in this country. However, some research suggests that marijuana is neither addictive nor a gateway drug and that it might actually benefit cancer and AIDS patients by reducing pain and encouraging failing appetites. Despite these findings and occasional legislative attempts to change the drug's status, marijuana remains illegal.

The Drug Education Library examines the paradox of drugs and drug use in America by focusing on some of the most commonly used and abused drugs or categories of drugs available today. By discussing objectively the many types of drugs, their intended purposes, their effects (both planned and unplanned), and the controversies surrounding them, the books in this series provide readers with an understanding of the complex role drugs and drug use play in American society. Informative sidebars, annotated bibliographies, and organizations to contact lists highlight the text and provide young readers with many opportunities for further discussion and research.

Introduction

"The Ugliest Drug There Is"

Methamphetamine is a potent and highly addictive drug. Although it has been illegally abused since the 1960s, when it was known as speed, during the 1980s a deadly new derivative, crystal meth, started to appear. One reason crystal meth quickly became popular is that it delivers a powerful high. Another is that the drug is inexpensive, because it is relatively easy to manufacture in basement drug labs, using products readily available at local pharmacies and grocery stores.

In 1999, U.S. Attorney General Janet Reno formed a task force to investigate what had become a meth epidemic in the United States. The task force warned, "Methamphetamine is a dangerous, addictive drug, and the population of users is not well defined and is expanding. . . . The clandestine laboratories where methamphetamine is produced domestically pose significant health hazards to law enforcement officials, nearby residents, and, through environmental hazards, the general public. Methamphetamine can be destructive to the human body, affecting neurological, behavioral, and psychological functioning long after use has stopped."[1]

In the United States today, people from many walks of life find themselves coming into contact with this dangerous drug. Police officers have certainly seen how methamphetamine can affect young people, as have prosecutors, judges, probation officers, and others who work in the criminal justice system. Additionally, social workers are faced with the problem of helping the children of parents who are addicted to meth. Firemen find themselves responding to house fires caused by the highly combustible process of cooking meth. Campers and hikers come across the toxic waste from meth labs, which is often dumped in the woods. Ordinary people are victims of identity theft—their credit card numbers stolen by crystal meth addicts desperate for money. Pharmacists catch shoplifters stealing cold medications that contain pseudoephedrine, a key ingredient needed to make the drug. Teachers look over their classrooms and see empty seats, their students missing school because of drug abuse.

Crystal methamphetamine is a dangerous and highly addictive drug that in recent years has grown more popular among young Americans.

In many cases, those people confronted with such situations will concede the fact that the meth epidemic caught them by surprise. They never realized it was such a problem until they found their credit card numbers stolen, responded to a fire at a meth lab, came across toxic chemicals dumped at their favorite campground, or had a friend die from an overdose of crystal meth.

The Effects of Crystal Meth

The narcotic effects of crystal meth are similar to those of cocaine but last much longer. Meth is a stimulant that affects the user's central nervous system. Meth users say they experience increased mental alertness and feelings of euphoria. Crystal users do not feel hungry or tired, and many will binge to extend the effects even further, smoking the drug continuously and staying awake for as long as fifteen days at a time.

Police officers in Washington, D.C., arrest a suspected drug dealer. Although police make many drug-related arrests, the flow of narcotics into the United States continues unabated.

Over the long term, people who use methamphetamine face a variety of physical effects as well as mental illnesses. Many of the chemicals used to manufacture methamphetamines were originally developed for industrial purposes and are, therefore, toxic. These chemicals can cause dangerous and often fatal effects. Additionally, the rise of meth use in the gay community has contributed to a re-emergence of HIV, the virus that causes the deadly disease AIDS. Mark A.R. Kleiman, a drug-policy expert at the University of California at Los Angeles, told a news reporter: "It's about the ugliest drug there is."[2]

Few young people realize how truly monstrous the drug can be. Crystal meth can become addictive after just a single use. Said Timothy, a teenager from Walnut Creek, California, "After the first time, I wanted it all the time. I thought I was so macho, I could do anything on it."[3]

The War Against Meth

Police are trying to shut down the meth labs that supply such users. Although some labs are located outside the United States, with the drugs then smuggled into the country, the main effort has focused on those who manufacture the drug inside U.S. borders. This effort often seems to be a never-ending battle. As Arkansas drug agent Danny Joe Ramsey remarked to a reporter in early 2004, "For every one meth lab we shut down, there are four others. I don't feel like we're making a dent."[4]

Part of the problem is that the key ingredient of meth—pseudoephedrine—finds its way into the United States from several countries, including Canada. Once the chemical arrives in the United States, it can be quickly synthesized into meth in an illegal lab. California is the location for many "superlabs"—operations that are capable of quickly producing large batches of the drug worth hundreds of thousands of dollars. In recent years, labs have spread throughout the Midwest and are now finding their way into the large cities on the East Coast. Many small-time labs are also operating in kitchens, basements, garages, and remote fields throughout the United States. With operations so widespread, information about manufacturing meth is readily available. For example, meth-making instructions and recipes are even posted on the Internet.

The ease with which crystal meth can be produced has caused great concern among experts on addiction. Mona Sumner, chief operating officer of Rimrock Foundation, a drug treatment center in Montana, voiced this frustration: "How are you going to cut off the supply of something that you can produce at home?"[5]

Still, there is hope. Federal officials have made the war against meth a national priority. Millions of dollars have been poured into anti-drug investigations targeted specifically at meth kingpins. On the local level, schools and community groups have started educating students about the dangers of meth addiction. The message may be getting through to young people—a 2004 study of teenagers' drug habits showed a decrease in meth use by students in the eighth and tenth grades. Meanwhile, legislators are taking steps they hope will place pseudoephedrine, which is available in over-the-counter cold medications, beyond the reach of illegal drug labs. Many experts are hopeful that these efforts will reduce or eliminate the growing problem of crystal meth abuse among young people in the United States.

Chapter 1

Speed Kills

When methamphetamine first came into widespread use in the 1960s, even people who abused other drugs condemned it, saying the drug caused bad trips, a terrible addiction, and even death. Still, methamphetamine became a much-abused narcotic, mostly because illegal laboratories could easily produce it. Today, notorious gangs operate clandestine laboratories that manufacture large quantities of methamphetamine. The drug, known as "ice," "crystal," or "meth," affects the lives of hundreds of thousands of people, whether in rural communities, comfortable suburbs, or crowded urban neighborhoods. Although recent evidence suggests that the drug may be losing popularity among young people, it still remains very much within their reach.

Development of a "Wonder Drug"

The story of methamphetamine begins in 1887, when a Japanese chemist named Nagayoshi Nagai extracted the active ingredient from the ephedra plant, creating a drug known as ephedrine. Within a few years, ephedrine would be put to use mainly as a treatment for asthma sufferers, helping to open their constricted

*Amphetamines commonly used today include Adipex (left), Dexedrine
(center), and Ritalin (right). Adipex is prescribed to treat obesity, while
the others are used to treat attention-deficit hyperactivity disorder
(ADHD) and narcolepsy.*

bronchial passages. It also would be used in nose drops, to clear
congestion in people with colds.

In the same year that Nagai made his discovery, a German
chemist named L. Edeleano combined ephedrine with other chemicals to make a drug known as amphetamine. This new drug was
also believed to be helpful for people with chest and nasal congestion. However, because it was time-consuming and difficult to
make, amphetamine was expensive, so doctors rarely prescribed it
for their patients. A breakthrough came in 1919, though, when
Japanese chemists found a quick and easy process to manufacture
amphetamine. In the process, they developed a new drug that took
the form of a crystalline powder. It could be taken in pill form, but
because it was soluble, meaning it could be dissolved in water, the
drug could also be administered to patients through injections.
The new drug became known as methamphetamine.

U.S. pharmaceutical companies soon began to market the new
drug to asthmatics under the names Desoxyn and Methedrine.
Meanwhile, new uses were being found for drugs classified as amphetamines. In 1927, for instance, it was discovered that amphetamines could raise a patient's blood pressure. This meant the
drugs might help patients with irregular heartbeats or otherwise
weak hearts. Amphetamines were also found to have stimulating
qualities—they could wake people up and make them more active. Other patients who responded well to amphetamines were
those who suffered from the rare disease known as narcolepsy.

These people, called narcoleptics, have trouble staying awake; they can fall asleep suddenly at any time of the day or night.

Amphetamines were also given to hyperactive, jittery children. Oddly, for these children the drugs had the opposite effect from what one would expect. Instead of making them more rambunctious, amphetamines calmed them and helped them concentrate.

Most people, however, took amphetamines to stay awake and have extra energy. During World War II, military leaders in Germany and the United States gave amphetamines to soldiers to help them stay alert during battles. The drugs were commonly used off the battlefields as well. College students used them to stay awake

Ma Huang

Some five thousand years ago, the Chinese discovered medicinal uses for the ephedra plant, known in China as ma huang. Ephedra is a shrub that grows about twenty inches high. The plant sprouts tiny leaves that soon shrivel up, but it features a tough and flexible stem that lasts for years. Typically, Chinese healers would brew the plant into a tea and serve it to their patients to treat colds and allergies. Ephedra is native to China but can also be found in India, Pakistan, Europe, the Middle East, North America, and South America.

Ephedrine can produce effects similar to those caused by adrenaline, the hormone that stimulates the heart and central nervous system, making muscles contract and blood pressure increase. Adrenaline produced under stress, many athletes believe, makes them perform better because the adrenaline rush makes their bodies stronger and faster. Yet while the effects of an adrenaline surge can be brief, the effects of ephedrine taken orally can be an adrenaline-like rush for an extended period of time. However, it can be dangerous. In 2003, Baltimore Orioles pitcher Steve Bechler, who was taking an ephedra-based dietary supplement, died from multiple organ failure and heat stroke. The dangers of ephedrine have prompted many professional sports associations, as well as the U.S. Olympic Committee, to place ephedrine on their lists of banned substances.

Among the common side effects of ephedrine abuse are insomnia, elevated blood pressure, increased pulse rate, anxiety, and headaches. Because ephedrine and its synthetic version, pseudoephedrine, are integral components of methamphetamine, the federal government and many state governments have restricted their availability.

all night so they could cram for tests. Truck drivers swallowed amphetamine pills to stay on the road longer. People also took amphetamines to help with dieting and to treat mild depression. Amphetamines seemed to be wonder drugs. By the 1950s, several American drug companies manufactured amphetamines and marketed them under dozens of names. Some of the drugs were available without a prescription.

From the time they were first created, amphetamines were abused. Users soon discovered that in addition to clearing up congestion and giving them energy, amphetamines could also provide a feeling of intoxication. During the 1920s, when alcohol was outlawed, some people turned to amphetamine pills as a substitute. During the Great Depression of the 1930s, when many people were out of work, amphetamines provided people with an easy escape from their troubles.

A new abuse of the drug surfaced in the 1950s. That is when soldiers stationed in Korea and Japan learned how to make and inject "speedballs"—a mixture of heroin and amphetamines. Back in the United States, this practice was basically unknown, so authorities did not suspect that soldiers returning from the Far East

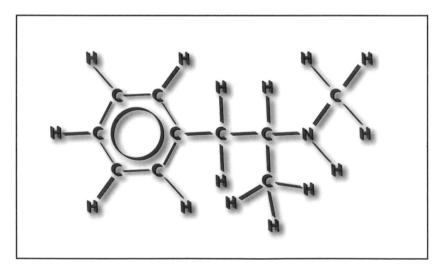

This diagram shows the chemical structure of Methamphetamine ($C_{10}H_{15}N$).

would be coming home with knowledge of a new and potentially devastating way to abuse drugs.

The Birth of Speed

In San Francisco during the 1950s, doctors started prescribing methamphetamine as a pain medication. One brand, Methedrine, became a particularly popular pain remedy, and because it was so cheap, patients preferred it to other pain medications. Soon, though, authorities started learning new information about methamphetamine. The drug's effects on the central nervous system were found to be far more intense than the effects of amphetamine. As with amphetamines, meth would perk up its users, giving them plenty of energy. But it also produced a hazy euphoria. The effects of methamphetamine lasted longer, too. The high provided by the drug could continue for ten hours or longer. Also, meth could cause users to turn violent and paranoid.

It did not take long for abusers of other drugs to turn to methamphetamine to get high. For example, many heroin abusers found San Francisco doctors willing to prescribe the drug to them, no questions asked. All they needed to do was scrape together a few dollars for an office visit and complain about pain to the doctor; after that they could walk out of the office with a prescription for Methedrine. One heroin addict told California drug researcher Dr. Roger C. Smith that he knew of unscrupulous doctors who would write prescriptions for Methedrine without even bothering to check whether the patients had needle marks in their arms from abusing heroin. He told Smith:

> There was a doctor . . . who would write anything for anybody at any time and he was making $7 a visit and on the day we went down there he wrote almost 400 prescriptions at $7 a head. So you can imagine how much money he was making. He made $2,800 that one day and they used to make caravans down there even from [Los Angeles] to his place. You'd get within two blocks of his office and you'd start seeing people you knew from all over.[6]

Pharmacies distributed Methedrine with few controls, some making it available in its injectable form without a prescription.

Two detectives dump amphetamine pills into an incinerator, in the 1960s. The pills were confiscated from service-station attendants convicted of selling them to truckers in Pennsylvania.

They would even provide the needles. With Methedrine so easy to obtain, many drug abusers decided to deal methamphetamine themselves. They would obtain the prescriptions, get them filled, and then sell the pills in various quantities to other addicts.

A crackdown occurred in 1963, when the federal government ordered drug manufacturers, physicians, and pharmacies to closely control the distribution of Methedrine as well as Desoxyn. As a result, sales of the two drugs became largely confined to hospitals, where the drugs were employed as surgical anesthesia. But that does not mean drug abusers stopped using methamphetamine. By that time, the techniques for making methamphetamine in unregulated "basement" labs had spread throughout the drug community. On the street, the drug became known as speed because of the frantic, energetic high it provided to its users and also because the drug could be manufactured quickly. Speed could be churned out in enormous quantities at a low cost.

"Frankenstein Speed Freaks"

Speed exploded onto the San Francisco drug scene in 1967, when thousands of young people flocked to Haight-Ashbury during what became known as the "Summer of Love." These young hippies were anxious to free themselves from the authority of their parents, teachers, and other members of the "establishment," and were willing to experiment with marijuana, LSD, and other drugs. One of the most readily available drugs was speed. For a few dollars, a young drug user could buy a dose of speed in its injectable form. Taking the drug through a needle came to be known as "shooting speed." People addicted to speed were known as "speed freaks."

During this period, some young people learned just how dangerous speed could be. Fatal overdoses were common, and soon warnings spread about the dangers of the drug. "Speed kills" became a common expression. Such cultural icons as the poet Allen Ginsberg and LSD proponent Timothy Leary as well as members of the Beatles and other musicians warned young people to stay away from speed. Ginsberg proclaimed in an interview with the *Los Angeles Free Press*, "Let's issue a general declaration to all the underground community. . . . Speed is antisocial, paranoid making, it's a drag, bad for your body, bad for your mind, generally speaking, in the long run uncreative and it's a plague in the whole dope industry. All the nice gentle dope fiends are getting screwed up by the real horror monster Frankenstein speed freaks who are going around stealing and bad mouthing everybody."[7]

In 1970, Congress adopted the U.S. Controlled Substances Act, making it illegal to possess or sell many drugs, including methamphetamine. A year later, President Richard M. Nixon made combating drug addiction a national priority. He declared a "War on Drugs," appointing a coordinator for all federal drug enforcement and prevention programs. Additionally, in 1973 Nixon established the Drug Enforcement Administration (DEA), making it the federal government's main weapon against drug traffickers.

The new, get-tough attitude on drugs soon produced results. In 1970, the year before Nixon declared the war on drugs, there were 415,000 narcotics-related arrests in the United States. Yet by 1972, only a year after the president's declaration, that number jumped to 527,000—more than a 25 percent increase. The numbers would continue to rise during the 1970s, reaching a peak of 642,000 by 1977.

One reason the police were making headway had to do with the nature of the manufacturing of the drug at that time. Because most speed labs were run by small-time, independent drug dealers, once police found a lab, it was easy for them to close it down and put the dealer out of business. That would soon change.

Biker Gangs Become Involved

Although the illegal methamphetamine business was affected by the crackdown, profits were so lucrative that those in the underground did not want to give up. Additionally, new players became involved. Outlaw motorcycle gangs got into the speed business during the 1970s and 1980s. Gangs such as the Hells Angels, Gypsy Jokers, and Warlocks, which had chapters in many American and Canadian cities, could establish a methamphetamine lab in one city and sell the drug in another. Under that scenario, even if police caught the street dealers, chances were they could provide little information on the location of the labs that were supplying them because only the roving gang members knew where to find the labs. A 1990 report on criminal activity by motorcycle gangs cited these findings:

> Law enforcement officials increasingly conclude that outlaw motorcycle gangs today are primarily narcotic networks, designed as continual crime-for-profit enterprises which gain their power through the use of fear and violence through their network of biker contacts. Their major money-making centers around the manufacture and distribution of methamphetamine and phencyclidine and the distribution of cocaine, marijuana and other illicit drugs. Methamphetamine was their most lucrative source of income in the early part of the decade [1980s.][8]

Occasionally, warfare among gangs broke out over turf in the lucrative meth market. Warring gangs committed murders and firebombed competing speed labs as they sought to dominate the

During the 1970s and 1980s, outlaw motorcycle gangs like the Hells Angels became involved in manufacturing and selling methamphetamines.

business. While the competition had fiercely intensified, this did not deter organized crime figures, who also decided to cash in on the methamphetamine business.

Still other changes occurred in this illegal drug trade. Until the late 1980s, the powerful ingredient in most of the illegal meth produced in the United States was the chemical phenyl-2-propanone, otherwise known as P2P. This chemical was used legally in industrial solvents and as an additive to pesticides, but for years the federal government had strictly regulated distribution of P2P. Still, there was a loophole: chemicals that could be combined to make P2P remained on the market, which meant they were available to the people operating illegal meth labs. To close the loophole, in

From Speed to Crystal

Speed is the version of methamphetamine that grew in popularity in the 1960s. It is far less potent than crystal meth, the form of the drug that is most often found today. That is a frightening fact, considering that speed is a truly dangerous drug, capable of killing a user who overdoses. What, then, makes crystal methamphetamine so much more potent, and what are its effects?

The potency of crystal meth can be attributed to the addition of hydrochloride—salt—to the mixture. The salt enables the meth to crystallize, so it can be smoked. When smoked, it affects the brain more severely than speed, which is typically swallowed rather than smoked.

Smoking crystal can provide a high within only ten seconds, whereas when methamphetamine is consumed by mouth, it can take up to thirty minutes for the effects to begin because the pill has to dissolve in the stomach. When smoked, the drug's vapors enter the lungs and are absorbed rapidly through the blood vessels lining the lungs; the meth is then carried quickly through the blood stream to the brain. Similarly, when a user injects a dose of methamphetamine into the body, the drug finds its way quickly to the brain. However, intravenous users sometimes miss their veins when they poke needles into their arms and get no high at all.

Techniques for cooking methamphetamine have improved since the 1960s, enabling labs to produce a much purer form of the drug. One such change in the manufacturing is the addition of anhydrous ammonia, a common farm fertilizer, to the cooking process. A lab that cooks crystal with anhydrous ammonia can produce a product that is 90 percent or more pure meth.

1988 the Drug Enforcement Administration placed the chemical components of P2P on its Chemical Diversion List, which meant the sale of the chemicals would be strictly controlled by law. With easy access to this potent ingredient cut off, it would seem that meth labs' operations would be stalled. Yet this was not the case; manufacturers of methamphetamine simply substituted ephedrine as the drug's principle component.

There was nothing new about cooking methamphetamine with ephedrine. Japanese chemists had first developed methamphetamine using ephedrine in 1919. And during World War II, chemists working in Germany perfected a quick manufacturing process by using ephedrine. This process became known as the "Nazi" cooking method, a term still in use today. Although ephedrine had also been placed on the Chemical Diversion List in 1988, drug makers found the substance far easier to find than P2P in the underground market. Also, as the meth lab operators would soon learn, when they were unable to find ephedrine, a much handier substitute was available on the shelves of every drug store in the United States, although using this substance would pose other challenges.

Cooking Crystal Meth

The federal government's crackdown on P2P and ephedrine did drive some gangs to establish meth labs in Mexico, where the importation of ephedrine was still legal. After cooking a batch of methamphetamine, the gang would smuggle it across the border into the United States, making it available to street dealers. Alternatively, Mexican drug dealers would simply smuggle the ephedrine into the United States, where it would be cooked into meth in American labs. Comparing the Mexican and American labs, California Bureau of Narcotics agent Brenda Heng told a reporter in 1994, "The Mexican labs we've seized have far greater production capabilities than the bikers ever dreamed of. And the stuff they're producing is 90 percent pure, which is amazing considering the filthiness of these labs. The bikers could never touch that kind of purity level."[9]

Meanwhile, a new type of meth was finding its way into the United States. At first, "crystal meth" or "ice" was smuggled into the United States from South Korea, Hong Kong, and the Philippines. Soon American lab operators learned the techniques for making crystal and began manufacturing it on their own. For this process, a supply of ephedrine is not essential; gangs found they could cook meth by substituting pseudoephedrine for ephedrine. Pseudoephedrine, a synthetic form of ephedrine, is a common ingredient found in many over-the-counter cold medicines.

While cold pills are readily available, it takes an enormous number to make methamphetamine—as many as seven hundred pills, each containing sixty grams of pseudoephedrine, to cook just an

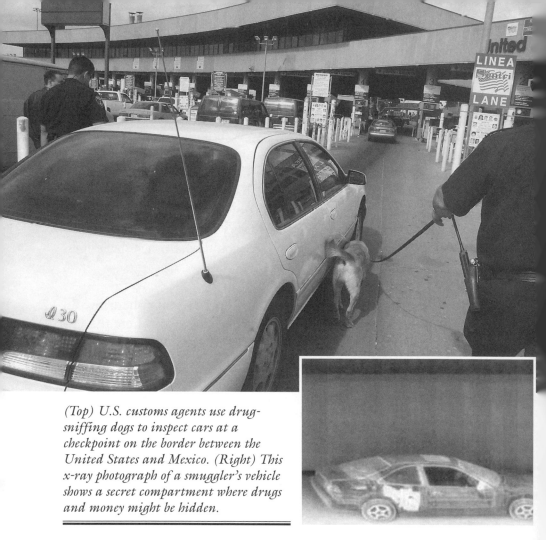

(Top) U.S. customs agents use drug-sniffing dogs to inspect cars at a checkpoint on the border between the United States and Mexico. (Right) This x-ray photograph of a smuggler's vehicle shows a secret compartment where drugs and money might be hidden.

ounce of methamphetamine. The typical box of cold medicine contains twenty-four pills. That means someone manufacturing methamphetamine has to find twenty-nine boxes of cold medicine just to make an ounce of the drug. A big-time lab, therefore, would require cartons and cartons of cold medicine. Since employees of many drug stores have been advised to call police if somebody buys more than a couple of boxes of cold medications, people involved in the manufacture of methamphetamine try to evade suspicion. They do a lot of driving from drug store to drug store. Illegal drug makers found they had to spend an enormous amount of time and effort rounding up the ingredients, but they also learned that pseudoephedrine cooked much faster than ephedrine. In fact, making methamphetamine with pseudoephedrine cuts the production time from several days to just a few hours.

After obtaining packages of the cold remedies, methamphetamine manufacturers cook the pills with various chemicals, including anhydrous ammonia, methanol, red phosphorous, lye, muriatic acid, and black iodine. All of these products are readily available in hardware stores or grocery stores.

Given the noxious nature of the chemicals involved, methamphetamine manufacturers find themselves enduring horrible odors while working in their labs. The smell that emanates from a meth brew is said to resemble that of cat urine. (Ironically, many manufacturers use kitty litter to filter the impurities out of the drug.) Finally, a solvent such as paint thinner must be stirred into the paste, which is then spread out to dry on a metal sheet. Chuck Allen, the chief of police in Granite Falls, Washington, bluntly told a reporter: "Battery acid, ammonia, paint thinner, lye—that's what you're smelling. Take a bunch of the most toxic solvents there are, mix 'em up with some Sudafed pills and put that in your pipe and smoke it. Your teeth'll fall out, your skin'll scab off, and

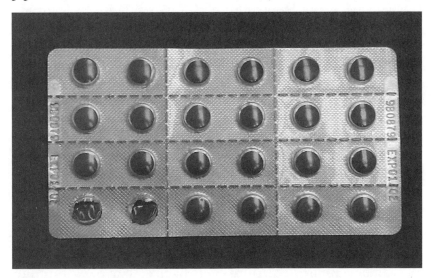

This package of cold medicine contains pseudoephedrine, a key ingredient in making methamphetamine.

a month from now you'll be coughing up chunks of your lung—but hey, what the hell? Party on, right?"[10]

After the paste dries for a few hours, it will coalesce into bright white or yellow crystals. The crystallization of the drug is the result of its high salt content. Crystal meth can be packed into the bowl of a pipe and smoked, crushed into a powder and snorted through the nose, swallowed in pill form, or boiled into a liquid and injected directly into the user's veins.

Enormous Profit Potential

For the illegal drug maker, the profit potential is enormous. In some California cities, street dealers may pay as much as $900 for an ounce of crystal meth. In turn, they will sell it to their customers for $100 a gram, or $150 for a purer form known as "glass." With about twenty-eight grams to the ounce, this means a street dealer can earn $2,800 or more by selling a single ounce of crystal. Of course, as with any illegal drug, the price varies from city to city and depends on the purity of the product, the quantity for sale, and the drug-abusing habits of the clientele.

The 2004 White House Office of National Drug Policy study known as *Pulse Check*, which tracked illegal drug use in twenty-five American cities, found that in Chicago users can expect to pay as much as $330 for a gram of crystal, while in New York City a gram of the drug costs a user $300. In Washington, D.C., a gram of crystal sells for $140, while in Cleveland, the street price is $75 per gram. In St. Louis, depending on the purity, a gram of methamphetamine sells for as little as $37. The report states, though, that meth dealers in the St. Louis area know they can charge as much as $100 for a gram of the drug in the suburbs, where the buyers are more affluent and are therefore willing to pay more.

It is hard to believe that most teenagers can afford such prices, but the evidence suggests that many young people are hooked on methamphetamine. To afford their habits, they plow through their savings, borrow money from their parents and friends, or steal. According to the 2003 *National Survey on Drug Use and*

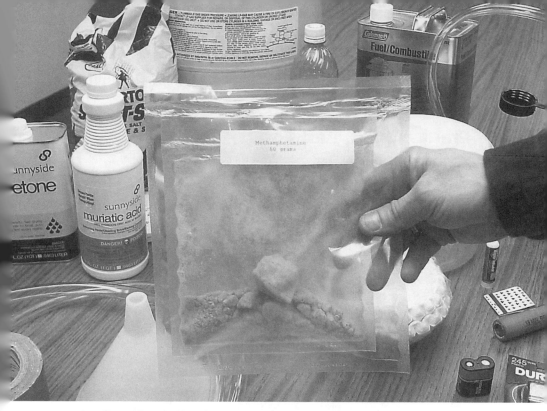

A police officer holds a bag containing close to 50 grams of methamphetamine. Behind the bag are some of the common household ingredients used to manufacture the drug.

Health conducted by the U.S. Substance Abuse and Mental Health Services Administration (SAMHSA), 12.3 million Americans over the age of twelve have used methamphetamine at least once in their lifetimes.

Some studies indicate, though, that use among young people may be declining. Each year, the University of Michigan issues its *Monitoring the Future* study, which gauges illegal drug use by students in the eighth, tenth, and twelfth grades. In late 2004, the study showed that among eighth- and tenth-grade students, meth use had declined during the previous twelve months. For eighth-grade students, there was a significant decline; the *Monitoring the Future* study reported that 1.5 percent of students in that age group used methamphetamine in 2004, down from 2.5 percent the year before. The drop in use among tenth-grade students was not as great; still, 3 percent of sophomores said they used the drug in 2004, down from 3.3 percent the year before. The *Monitoring*

Crank, Chalk, and Cat

Back in the 1960s, people who used methamphetamine were known as "speed freaks." Now, such users are often called "tweakers," and smoking the drug is known as "tweaking."

Methamphetamine earned the nicknames "crystal" and "ice" because of the effects of its salt content. The salt, or hydrochloride, used in making crystal meth is what causes it to form into white or yellow rock-like chunks and take on the crystal or ice-like appearance. A particularly pure batch of crystal is called "glass" or simply "G." Other street names for the drug are "bikers' coffee," "chalk," "chicken feed," "crank," "cristy," "go-fast," "methlies quick," "poor man's cocaine," "shabu," "speed," "stove top," "trash," "yellow barn," and "zip."

In Thailand, a tablet of methamphetamine combined with caffeine—the stimulant found in coffee—is known as "yaba." In recent years, yaba tablets have been found circulating in Asian communities in California.

And in some Midwestern states, including Michigan and Wisconsin, a potent drug similar to methamphetamine known as methcathinone has surfaced as an abused substance. Methcathinone provides a high similar to methamphetamine, but the active ingredient is cathinone rather than pseudophedrine. Cathinone is extracted from the khat plant, the leaves of which are illegally imported into the United States from Yemen and Ethiopia as well as other Middle East and African countries. Chewing khat leaves provides a modest high. When the cathinone is extracted from the plant, it can provide a potent ingredient. As with methamphetamine, methcathinone requires the use of toxic chemicals. Known as "cat," "goob," and "morning star," methcathinone can be manufactured in a basement lab with solvents available at any hardware store.

the Future authors said the lower numbers of eighth- and tenth-grade students admitting to using methamphetamine continued a five-year trend showing a decline in the drug's use by students in those age groups.

The number of twelfth-grade students who reported using methamphetamine in 2004 increased from 2003. In 2004, 3.4 percent of high school seniors said they used methamphetamine, while in 2003, just 3.2 percent admitted to using the drug. Although this was the first increase in meth use among high-school seniors since 1999, the upward trend concerns drug researchers.

Stephanie Mauth, a juvenile probation officer in Moffat County, Colorado, told a news reporter that methamphetamine had become the "drug of choice" among many young people who are reaching the end of their high school years. She explained, "It's significant here and it's increasing. It used to be pot, but now it seems to be meth use. . . . From age 16 on up is the most popular age range. It's the time when youth start intermingling with young adults. It's easier for them to network and get the drug."[11]

And so methamphetamine use by young people remains a concern of educators, parents, social workers, and government officials. According to the 2004 *Pulse Check* report:

> At an adolescent facility in Los Angeles, females coming into treatment are nearly all primary methamphetamine users. In Minneapolis/St. Paul, high school counselors are reporting use by younger age groups. In Sacramento, the percentage of young adults among methamphetamine users has increased, while the percentage of older adults has declined. Some Hispanic adolescents in New York are snorting methamphetamine . . . purchased from one young man selling it in $20 packets.[12]

There is no question that meth is more available today than even ten years ago. The 2004 *Monitoring the Future* study reported that 19.5 percent of tenth-grade students believe crystal meth is available to them. In 1994, 17.8 percent of high school sophomores said that crystal meth is a drug they find available. What is more, the Drug Enforcement Administration says that in 1994, police in America closed down 263 meth labs. By contrast, in 2003, DEA reported that police closed down 9,368 meth labs. Interviewed by a reporter, California DEA agent Jack Hook explained, "You can go into any school in San Diego County and ask what 'crystal' is, and many will be able to tell you, and also where to get it. That's how prevalent it is here."[13]

Fighting a Lifetime Addiction

Young people who use methamphetamine hope to achieve a high that can last as long as twelve hours. They believe the drug will make them feel good about themselves. If they are overweight, meth makes them feel slim. If they are depressed, meth makes them feel happy. If they are lonely, well, they are sure to find plenty of people their own age willing to share a bowl of crystal.

And yet, young people who experiment with meth risk becoming addicted to a drug that can cause violent behavior, confusion, and insomnia. They risk suffering from the mental illness known as paranoia, which can cause suicidal or even homicidal thoughts. What is more, use of methamphetamine can create numerous physical problems, including brain damage, convulsions, stroke, heart disease, and death. Stephanie Mauth, the Colorado probation officer, explained, "The problem is, if you've experienced it once like a kid, injecting meth at 16, you're talking about a lifelong addiction. If they're taking it when they're young, they have the rest of their lives to fight it."[14]

Chapter 2

The Physical Effects of Methamphetamine

For methamphetamine users, the physical and psychological effects of the drug begin with their first puffs from the crystal meth pipe. The drug enters the lungs and is metabolized into the blood stream, where it rushes into the brain and produces an immediate feeling of euphoria, or great joy. Yet as users take larger and more frequent doses, they risk severe and long-lasting consequences that can lead to mental illness as well as physiological problems that include brain damage, convulsions, stroke, heart disease, and death. Users are not the only victims of the drug. Indeed, just being in the vicinity of meth production has proven to be fatal for some. In addition, unsafe sexual contact by people under the influence of crystal meth is responsible for a resurgence in the deadly virus that causes AIDS.

The Methamphetamine High
Immediately after drawing in the smoke from a bowl of crystal meth, or injecting liquid methamphetamine into a vein, the user will experience a rush or flash that will last a few minutes. With every new hit of the drug, the flash of pleasure will be repeated. But that is not the end of the experience. The high produced by

A teenage girl prepares to smoke crystal meth by cooking it in a glass pipe.

methamphetamine has been compared to that of cocaine. But while cocaine's effects start wearing off after twenty or thirty minutes, even a small dose of methamphetamine will have effects that last for eight hours or more as the general feeling of euphoria lingers on. Larger doses, which are consumed by habitual users, can last more than twenty-four hours. Methamphetamine addiction researcher Dr. John C. Kramer described the first hit of the drug as an "ecstatic experience," and said the user's first thought is, "Where has this been all my life?"[15]

Smoking and injecting methamphetamine are the most popular forms of ingesting the drug because they provide the fastest ways for users to get high. Those who snort the drug must wait three to five minutes for the high to take effect. Those who swallow the drug in pill form will find it can take as long as twenty minutes to gain a feeling of euphoria.

Methamphetamine is not physically addictive, but its users find themselves psychologically addicted. Because the body quickly builds up a resistance to the drug, users must seek stronger and more frequent doses to achieve the same euphoric high. In a study of meth addiction published in the *Journal of Psychedelic Drugs*, Kramer wrote:

> It takes ever more drug to recreate this chemical nirvana. It is the desire to re-experience the flash and the desire to remain euphoric, and to avoid the fatigue and the depression of the "coming down," which drives the users to persist and necessarily to increase their dose and frequency of injection. And it is this persistence of use and these large doses which bring on all the other effects of these drugs.[16]

Abusers frequently binge: they will keep smoking bowl after bowl of crystal, so they can stay high for days at a time. During this time, they do not sleep or eat. Malea Gowins, who was jailed for cooking meth in Craig, Colorado, told a newspaper reporter, "The amount of drugs I was inserting into my system right before I went to prison is just baffling to me. I was doing more than an eight ball [of methamphetamine] a day by myself . . . which is three and a half grams. . . . I was a mess. I was in a bad, bad way."[17]

Changes to the Brain

When users ingest methamphetamine, they introduce a drug to their brains that affects release of a neurotransmitter known as dopamine. Neurotransmitters are the chemicals that carry messages from brain cell to brain cell. For example, the messages may tell a foot to take a step, or a hand to hold a pencil, or the lips to form words so that the person may speak. Dopamine is the neurotransmitter that enables the body to move and that also regulates emotions, particularly the feeling of pleasure. Methamphetamine causes the brain to release more dopamine. This is what makes a meth user feel good.

Constant use of methamphetamine will permanently change the user's brain. For instance, when too much dopamine is artificially stimulated by methamphetamine or another substance, the brain responds by making less dopamine on its own. This means that heavy meth users may find it hard to feel happy during the periods when they are not under the influence of the drug. This drop in the brain's natural dopamine level has even more serious consequences for the long term. Recent scientific studies have suggested that when the brain stops making dopamine on its own, the brain cells that transmit the chemical are affected. Research shows the nerve endings of the cells, which are known as terminals, are cut back and generally do not grow back to full size. This effect on brain cells has suggested to medical researchers that methamphetamine can lead to Parkinson's disease—a severe disorder that causes rigid muscles, tremors in the fingers and hands, and garbled speech. In recent years, long-time methamphetamine users have exhibited such symptoms.

Other Problems

People who consume methamphetamine must also deal with a host of other problems. Meth users are highly alert, aggressive, and in constant motion. (This is why some forms of the drug are called "speed.") Often, they are unable to sleep. Meth users can also become irritable and confused, or engage in compulsive behavior. "I have seen patients tie and retie a shoelace hundreds of times, striving for the perfect knot,"[18] said Dr. Herbert D. Kleber of the Center on Addiction and Substance Abuse at Columbia University in New York.

Heavy, prolonged use of methamphetamine can lead to much more severe forms of mental illnesses, such as anxiety and paranoia. People who are paranoid become fearful of others, both strangers and people they know well. They do not trust their friends and may believe their lives are in danger. Barbara Zugor, director of the Treatment Assessment Screening Center in Phoenix, Arizona, described symptoms of the heavy, long-time abuser to a news reporter: "They have hallucinations, delusionary thoughts. They're not really in their right state of mind, and they have not been eating properly, drinking properly. They're really in a total state of confusion, and so, therefore, their thinking pat-

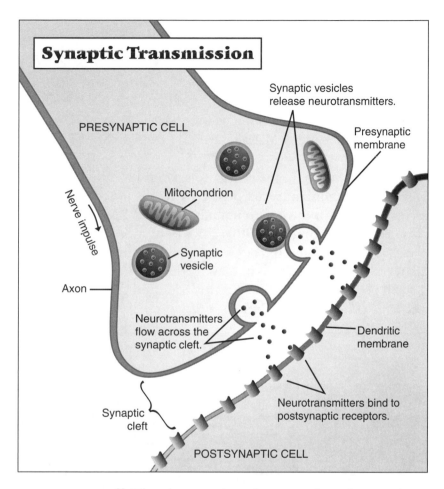

terns are way off. They have no impulse control, and many times they think people are after them."[19]

People who are in a drug-induced state of paranoia can be dangerous to themselves and others. One user told drug abuse researcher Dr. Richard C. Smith about a meth-abusing friend:

> He's a very nice person, and extremely generous; however, when he gets all jacked up and he is wired [stimulated with speed] . . . then he is in trouble. Because pretty quick he's got a shotgun and everybody else has got a shotgun. I've seen him out in front of . . . the freeway entrance herding the hitch-hikers away because he's paranoid of them. At four o'clock in the afternoon, with a full length shotgun, he's screaming, "Move on, you can't stand there, move on." That's just the way he gets.[20]

New AIDS Menace

Methamphetamine also affects the area of the brain known as the limbic cortex. This is the part of the brain that controls fear and hostility as well as hunger and sex drive. The drug causes its users to desire sex and ignore the need for food. "You don't care about eating, clean clothes, bathing, as long as you're getting high," explained former addict Malea Gowins. "I lived on SweeTarts and Gatorade."[21]

Users find they have the energy to stay up for days, and many of them crave constant sexual activity. This has led to widespread use of the drug in the gay community, where "PNP" parties became popular during the 1990s ("PNP" stands for "party and play," meaning drugs and sex.) In 2003, Hunter College conducted a study of gay men in New York City, in which it found that 20 percent of male homosexuals had used crystal meth. Because the drug erases inhibitions, many users have spontaneous,

In recent years, use of crystal meth has become very popular among young gay men.

unprotected sexual encounters. This has contributed to an increase in HIV infections among gay men.

HIV causes acquired immune deficiency syndrome (AIDS), a disease that spread in epidemic proportions, particularly among gay men, during the 1980s. However, an intense and widespread public education program about the dangers of AIDS led many people to exercise caution before having sex, which helped reduce the spread of the deadly virus. The U.S. Centers for Disease Control and Prevention reported in 2001, "As a result of . . . HIV prevention efforts and increases in societal awareness of and response to the AIDS epidemic, new infections in the United States, which had risen rapidly to a peak of 150,000 per year in the mid-1980s, declined to an estimated 40,000 per year since 1992."[22]

Presently, however, the use of crystal meth by homosexuals has caused many gay activists to believe AIDS once again poses a widespread threat, not only because gay men can spread the disease through unprotected sex, but also because HIV can be spread by sharing intravenous needles, which are used to inject liquid meth. The Centers for Disease Control said that HIV infections among gay men rose some 11 percent between 2000 and 2003.

Peter Staley, a gay rights activist and former crystal meth user, said many gays use methamphetamine because it provides a release from the stigma they feel as homosexuals. "We're dealing with [the] fact that for most of our adult lives we have been sexual pariahs, tainted goods because of our HIV status, and all of a sudden we find a drug that takes that away," he told a reporter. "You feel young again when you're high. All those negative feelings you've been carrying around disappear. It was the perfect escape, and I'm not making any excuses for it. I'm just trying to explain why in that demographic I think it took off so quickly."[23]

Ultimately, however, crystal meth creates problems, rather than solving them. In 2005, officials of the New York State Health Department announced discovery of a new strain of HIV that resists treatment by drugs that have been available to AIDS patients for more than a decade. The victim of the new HIV strain was a gay man who used crystal meth regularly and had numerous sexual partners. "We're seeing new infections that already, one, two, three or four medications can't be used to treat,"[24] said Gal Mayer, associate medical director of Callen-Lorde Community Health Center in New York, which provides treatment to gay patients.

Overdoses Are Common

A dose of methamphetamine causes the user's blood pressure to rise. The pulse starts racing, and, often, the heartbeat is irregular. Users also experience hyperthermia—an increase in body temperature. When too much meth is taken, these symptoms can be fatal. In 2002, hospitals reported treating nearly 18,000 people in meth overdose cases.

The drug damages blood vessels in the brain, which can lead to stroke. An overdose of methamphetamine also can cause death from heart failure, and some meth users have died after lapsing into uncontrollable seizures or convulsions. "An overdose with crystal meth or any amphetamine could lead to a sudden death, no doubt," said Dr. Charl Els, a psychiatrist in Edmonton, Canada, who often treats meth abusers. Els said that a meth sufferer experiencing a seizure can stop breathing and suffer a heart

---

Meth Mites and Crank Bugs

People who use methamphetamine often find themselves suffering from a psychiatric condition known as formication: the belief that tiny bugs are crawling along their skin. In reality, the bugs do not exist. Users call these imaginary bugs "meth mites" or "crank bugs."

Formication is caused by the toxic additives used to make crystal meth. When the body fails to digest the additives, it rejects them by forcing the chemicals out of the meth user's pores. The condition causes itching. Since meth use also causes a rise in body temperature and sweating, the itching can become intense. At this point, the meth user is usually deep within the throes of a drug binge and believes the itching is caused by tiny bugs. The user scratches incessantly, which usually causes sores. Because meth users tend to ignore personal hygiene, they often have dirty fingernails, which means they risk infection if they scratch open sores. Even after meth users kick their habits, they may carry permanent scars caused by scratching the imaginary meth mites.

Meth Mouth

Dentists can often tell whether patients are meth users: their teeth are usually ground down and black with decay. Many of them develop gum disease.

There are many reasons methamphetamine users get what is known as "meth mouth." For starters, methamphetamine causes dry mouth in its users. With little saliva in their mouths, meth users have no natural protection against the acids in the drug that enter their mouths when they smoke crystal.

To quench their thirsts, many meth users reach for soft drinks, which are often high in caffeine and laden with sugar. Also, the anxiety and paranoia caused by the drug prompts many of its users to grind their teeth. Most meth users lose interest in personal hygiene, so they do not brush their teeth or visit their dentists. Deborah Durkin, an environmental scientist for the Minnesota Health Department, told the *St. Paul Pioneer Press*, "All these factors enter into it, and it is very, very common for there to be infections and tooth loss."

Jassen Ferris, a thirty-one-year-old former meth user and inmate in a Minnesota prison, told the newspaper that meth abuse cost him several of his teeth. "I'm in a lot of pain," he revealed. "If I eat an apple, like, pieces of my teeth will break off. My early 20s were when I first started getting problems with my teeth. . . . If I had a toothache, I'd smoke more and it killed the pain. When you are using meth, you use any excuse you can to use some more."

Meth mouth is a condition in which the user's teeth rot due to lack of saliva.

attack. "People can die, just literally in the blink of an eye,"[25] he explained.

Meth users who share needles face a separate set of health issues. In addition to HIV, needle-sharing meth users risk contracting a number of communicable diseases, including hepatitis, a

DON'T LET DRUG DEALERS CHANGE
THE FACE OF YOUR NEIGHBOURHOOD.
Call Crimestoppers anonymously on 0800 555 111.

This British antidrug poster poignantly illustrates the physical effects of methamphetamine. The woman, who was addicted to meth, is pictured at age 36 (above) and 40 (below).

virus that causes an inflammation of the liver. Staphylococcus infections are also common among meth users; because meth users typically have open sores from scratching their itchy skin, when they come into contact with other users' bodies—often during sex—staph infections can be spread from wound to wound. Staph can cause boils and other skin ailments, and if left untreated the disease can spread to vital organs.

In addition, a meth user can suffer burns and permanent damage to the throat and esophagus—the tube that leads to the stomach. The cause of such damage is drain cleaner, a common ingredient of crystal methamphetamine because it contains acids necessary to make the drug. When the drain cleaner enters the body, it eats away the tissue. It can permanently damage a meth user's ability to speak or digest food.

A Drug that Destroys Lives

Donna Green believes her meth addiction nearly cost her life. After graduating in 1993 from a high school in Terre Haute, Indiana, Green went on to college, where she discovered methamphetamine. For the next ten years, Green used methamphetamine off and on: binging on meth when she could find it and ingesting other substances, such as prescription drugs and cocaine, as they were available. She told a newspaper reporter, though, that meth was her drug of choice. She enjoyed injecting the drug while in her bathroom; Green would lock the door and keep a television set or stereo playing as she got high. Sometimes, she would remain in the bathroom for days. During this time Green gave birth to four babies, taking meth during all four of her pregnancies.

By 2001, Green was hospitalized with a leaky heart valve and a staph infection. She was also diagnosed with hepatitis. Green needed to breathe with the assistance of a respirator and soon slipped into a coma. Her doctor wrote, "Her prognosis is not good."[26] Family members planned her funeral.

Green emerged from the coma after two months. She woke to find herself connected to a feeding tube, and unable to walk or talk. By 2003, Donna Green found herself living in hospitals and nursing homes as she slowly regained use of her body. The right side of her face is still numb. Purple bruises remain under her arms—the scars that are left after years of sticking needles into her veins. Her skin is pale. She has trouble remembering and finds it difficult to maneuver a pencil. When a reporter asked how old she felt, the twenty-seven-year-old former meth user answered, "Seventy."[27]

Crank Babies

Pregnant women who use meth do not just harm themselves when they abuse the drug. Meth can cause permanent damage to their unborn children. Women who use meth during their pregnancies risk delivering their babies prematurely, which can lead to birth defects or health problems. Also, lead acetate is often used in the methamphetamine cooking process, and the lead remains in the crystal after it hardens. This means meth users can find themselves suffering from lead poisoning, which in adults can cause increased blood pressure, sterility, muscle and joint pain, and memory loss. Pregnant women also risk poisoning their babies with lead. Because the brains and bodies of young children are still in the formative stages, a baby suffering from lead poisoning may face a reduced IQ, learning disabilities, attention deficit disorders, behavioral problems, stunted growth, impaired hearing, and kidney damage. At high levels of exposure, a child may become mentally retarded, fall into a coma, and even die from lead poisoning. "These mothers, by using methamphetamine, may be condemning kids to a lifetime of disability,"[28] said Dr. Rizwan Shah of Blank Children's Hospital in Des Moines, Iowa. Over eight years, Dr. Shah studied 368 "crank babies"—children born to mothers addicted to methamphetamine.

Babies born to mothers addicted to methamphetamine are not born addicted to the drug. However, within the first twenty-four hours the infants can develop seizures related to the toxic chemicals in their bodies. Dr. Shah explained that even though the drug will clear out of their brains within three days, the toxic effects of meth on their bodies last much longer. Within the first month of birth, these babies are in danger of developing heart and respiratory problems. They are also at elevated risk for strokes. Shah reported that "those babies that survive this kind of catastrophe continue to struggle. Beyond the first month of life, they show signs of brain toxicity."[29]

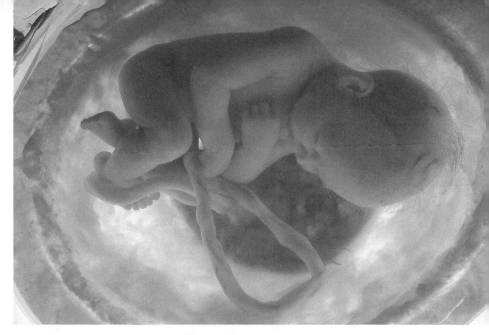

When pregnant women use methamphetamine, their babies are often born with a host of physical and developmental problems.

Crank babies sleep for as much as twenty-three hours a day. Their bodies might be as limp as a dish rag, according to Shah. Crank babies experience rapid breathing spells, and they have trouble swallowing and sucking, which all babies must do to drink milk or formula. Their fingers and toes often tremble. According to Shah, meth babies do not like to be touched.

Shah has also seen children who are growing up in homes where meth use and meth making is common. In these cases, she said, the children's mothers may not have used methamphetamine during their pregnancies; nevertheless, the children are exposed to the toxic fumes—such as anhydrous ammonia and ether—that are found in most meth labs. Shah said she finds these children hyperactive and irritable. And in many cases, Shah said, the children have high levels of lead content in their bodies.

Volatile Compounds

For decades federal and state authorities have tried to prevent lead from being released into the environment, banning the use of lead in many consumer products, including house paint and gasoline. When lead and other toxic substances are employed in industry, government agencies such as the Environmental Protection

Firefighters examine the charred remains of a meth superlab in Madera County, California. In the foreground is a huge pile of crushed cans of denatured alcohol, which is used in the manufacturing process.

Agency and the Occupational Safety and Health Administration have established strict rules about the levels of the substances that are permitted in the workplace. In most cases, expensive ventilation and air-scrubbing equipment has to be employed to protect the health of the factory workers as well as the health of the people who live near the plant.

But the typical meth lab owner cares little about venting the noxious fumes from the work area, even though the production of meth requires the use of solvents and other toxic chemicals. As a result, people who cook meth subject themselves to a variety of fumes that can cause brain damage, liver and kidney failure, cancer, birth defects, and sterility. But the physical dangers of the meth lab do not stop there. Because the meth-making process involves a number of volatile compounds, explosions and fires in meth labs are common.

Malea Gowins was nearly killed while cooking meth. In her case, Gowins said, she thought she was being careful—setting up the lab in the middle of a remote field. Still, the volatile mix exploded, and Gowins found herself immersed in flames. "I was on fire," she told a reporter. "There was battery acid and paint thinner all over me. I was literally on fire. My coat was on fire and stuff." Luckily, Gowins said, she had brought along a jug of water and baking soda. "I just dumped it over my head and just tore my clothes off. I'm out in this cornfield, of course, stripping down, on fire. That was awful."[30]

Deadly Meth Lab Fires

Gowins was lucky. She survived the fire. Others have not been as fortunate. In 1997, three-year-old Michael Carnesi died while asleep in his mother's Phoenix apartment; police alleged he inhaled deadly fumes from a batch of meth that was cooking in the kitchen. And in late 1995, a mobile home in remote Aguanga, California, burst into flames when a meth lab inside the dwelling exploded. Kathy James, her seven-year-old son Jimmy, and at least six men inside the home made it out safely, but three of James's children—Dion, three; Jackson, two; and Megan, one—died in the fire. When police and fire officials arrived at the scene, witnesses told them that James, who had been burned in the fire, at first told them not to contact authorities. Witnesses also said that none of the men who ran out of the home tried to save the young children inside.

After the deadly blaze, James was charged with three counts of murder. Ed Synicky, special agent in charge of the California Bureau of Narcotics office in nearby Riverside, told a reporter, "These people are focused on manufacturing drugs for their personal use and profit, and safety—whether for their own lives, their children or their neighbors—is a secondary concern of theirs."[31]

A Steep Price to Pay

For most methamphetamine users, the price they pay for getting high is steep. They risk damaging their brains and vital organs and even death from an overdose or from getting trapped in a meth lab fire. Many users pay the price with a lifetime of mental illness. Additionally, the damage they can do to their lives goes far beyond physical problems and psychiatric illness. Meth addicts stop caring about their jobs. Young people who use meth lose interest in school, in getting good grades, and in gaining admission to college. They care only about obtaining their next bowl of crystal.

Meth users abuse other people as well. The families and friends of meth users suffer while a loved one drifts further and further into addiction. Even strangers pay the price for meth addiction; many of them are the victims of crimes committed by methamphetamine addicts who are too high to control their actions, which was perhaps the case in Aguanga. Synicky voiced hope: "Maybe the legacy of the three James children can wake up the country to the dangers of methamphetamine. I sure hope so."[32]

 # Chapter 3

The Effect of Methamphetamine on Society

Methamphetamine addiction affects both the drug user and the people around him or her. Addicts care little about their families, their futures, their educations, or their jobs. They find themselves in an endless spiral of abuse, concerned only about finding their next hit of crystal meth. They often turn to crime to support their habits or, while under the influence of the drug, commit crimes against innocent victims. The drug affects society in other ways as well. Residents of neighborhoods where labs are located are at risk for fires or explosions, and the toxic chemicals used in the manufacture of the drug pollute the nearby environment.

When Family Members Are Addicted

Methamphetamine takes a particularly devastating toll on the lives of young people. One example is Ann Marie de Lathouder, a fourteen-year-old honor student from Waterbury, Iowa. For six months, Ann Marie's mother Ellen noticed her daughter losing weight, neglecting her personal hygiene, and acting moody. Ann Marie's grades were also slipping; the one-time A student was now carrying a D average. Finally, the mother of one of Ann Marie's friends approached Ellen and told her she suspected their daughters were using drugs.

Ellen de Lathouder searched through her daughter's room and soon found a locked box containing leaves of charred tinfoil, a telltale sign of methamphetamine use because crystal is often sold rolled up in foil. She also found a poem about meth in her daughter's journal of poetry:

> Try it once and then you'll see, how willingly you'll pay its fee. I tell you now, don't even start, you'll loathe the jumping of your heart; For a while you might love everyone, but no one matters when you're looking for some; Now you're awake while they're all sleeping, you should be laughing so why are you weeping?[33]

Ellen and her ex-husband Frank confronted Ann Marie. They learned that their daughter had been snorting, smoking, and even eating crystal meth for some six months. She had developed a habit that cost $30 a day and financed it with her lunch money, her allowance, and cash she raised by selling her books and CDs. Ann Marie disclosed to her parents that she discovered crystal during a New Year's Eve party. "I thought it would be fun," she told

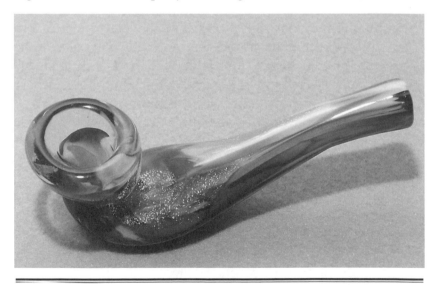

Some meth users acquire fancy paraphernalia, like this hand-blown glass pipe for smoking the drug.

Methamphetamine can be found both as a crystal (called "ice" or "glass") and powder ("crank" or "speed").

a reporter. "At that time, I wanted to do anything and everything I could get."[34]

The de Lathouders forced their daughter to enter a drug treatment program, but participating in the program was no easy experience for Ann Marie. She fought the treatment, refused to take drugs prescribed to control the depression caused by her addiction, and went through terrible withdrawal symptoms while trying to give up crystal. Additionally, she started drinking alcoholic beverages to try to compensate for the loss of meth from her life. She was arrested for public drunkenness, and when taken into custody, police determined she had consumed almost a lethal amount of alcohol. She was hospitalized, and the near-fatal experience prompted Ann Marie to dedicate herself to giving up substance abuse. After her release from the hospital, the teenager reentered a drug addiction program, successfully kicked her habit, and returned to high school.

The experience devastated the de Lathouders, forcing them to live with their daughter's addiction and suffer while searching for ways to convince her to give up drugs. "You don't want to think

Signs of Meth Use

Young people can look for signs of meth use in their friends. For starters, meth users often lose weight very quickly. While using the drug, a meth abuser will sweat a great deal, especially around the eyebrows and lips. Because methamphetamine raises a person's blood pressure, blood vessels in the face are often constricted, which produces a pale and sickly complexion.

Under the influence of the drug, people may stagger or stumble and otherwise exhibit poor coordination. Their speech may be slurred. Meth users do not sleep much. They also lose interest in personal hygiene.

The meth user will undergo a number of other changes as well. In the beginning, most meth users are in a constant state of euphoria, yet they soon become irritable, anxious, and aggressive. They seem to be in constant motion. Eventually, they become paranoid and suspect that their friends and family members would like to harm them.

If a meth user takes an overdose of the drug, symptoms may include shallow breathing, clammy skin, and eye pupils that are dilated, meaning they are open wide. Their pulse may be weak or rapid. Because meth users can be dangerous if approached, experts recommend that people who suspect a friend or family member has overdosed should not try to provide first-aid themselves but should instead call police or an ambulance squad.

your child is using drugs," Ellen de Lathouder said. "It's better not to see the evidence. But I remember looking into Ann Marie's eyes, and it was like she didn't have a soul."[35]

Destroying Families

Ann Marie was fortunate; her parents found out about her drug abuse in time and forced her to enter a rehabilitation program. The families of Janelle Hornickel and Michael Wamsley were not so lucky. The 20-year-olds were on their way to their Omaha, Nebraska, apartment in early January 2005, when they were caught in a snowstorm. Over the next few hours, the two young people called 911 several times, asking for help because they were lost. Because they were calling from a cellular phone, the 911 dispatcher could not pinpoint where they were; he could only tell the location of the nearest cell tower. The calls became more and more bizarre and frantic as the night went on. Then the calls stopped.

During the night, temperatures dropped below 0° Fahrenheit (–18° Celsius). The next day, searchers found Wamsley's body; a week later, Hornickel's body was discovered. Both were lightly dressed, and had frozen to death.

At first, investigators did not understand why the couple had left their truck during the storm. When it was found, the truck still had half a tank of gas, as well as warm clothes and a cell phone. The two bodies were less than two miles from the truck when they were found. Police had a better idea when they discovered a small quantity of crystal meth in the truck, and autopsy reports showed that both of the deceased young people had taken the drug the night they died. Dr. Henry Nipper, director of toxicology at

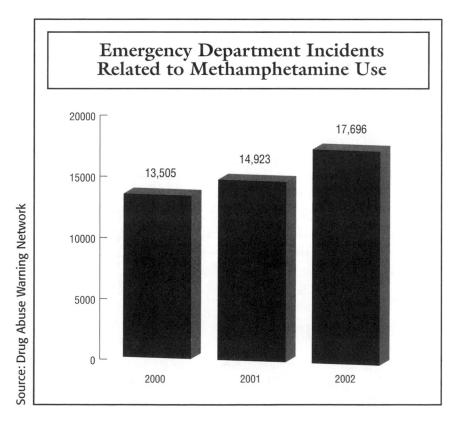

Emergency Department Incidents Related to Methamphetamine Use

Source: Drug Abuse Warning Network

Creighton University Medical Center, said the methamphetamines the two had ingested could cause confusion and anxiety and would have impaired their judgment and ability to feel the cold weather.

"It makes you angry from a lot of aspects," Sarpy County Chief Deputy Sheriff Jeff Davis said. "Two people lost their lives. Two families are going through and will continue to go through a terribly traumatic ordeal. Secondary to that [is] the expense to taxpayers; the volunteers, the danger they were put in."[36]

Sometimes a meth user is a parent, and so the addiction tears a family apart in other ways. In 2001, Shawn Hinrichs, twenty-four, was arrested with three other people for running a meth lab in a campground near Rochester, Minnesota. She pleaded guilty and was sentenced to sixty days in jail followed by a stay in a halfway house, a residential facility for drug abusers. As the resident of a halfway house, Hinrichs was not permitted to care for her three children. The children's father, Hinrichs' boyfriend, was also unable to care for the children, because he was serving an eight-year term on meth-related charges in a Minnesota prison. Under the rules of the Minnesota Department of Corrections, Hinrichs is prohibited from taking the children to see their father until she remains off drugs for at least a year. Ultimately, the father will not be able to become a part of his children's lives until he is released from jail.

A journalist found Hinrichs' mother, Kathy Anderson, caring for her three grandchildren, whose ages ranged from three to seven. Anderson said she had to give up her job to become a stay-at-home mother. During a visit to her mother's house, Shawn Hinrichs watched her three children play. "I don't know when I'm going to get this family back together,"[37] Hinrichs said.

Devastating Impact

The stories of Ann Marie de Lathouder, Janelle Hornickel, Michael Wamsley, and Shawn Hinrichs are typical of the lives of methamphetamine users. Their circumstances and those of others show that crystal meth is not just a problem found in cities. Fami-

Fertilizer Thieves

Meth lab operators use the chemical anhydrous ammonia to make crystal, adding it to their methamphetamine recipes so that the pseudoephedrine, also in the mixtures, forms into a paste. While used illegally by these operators, anhydrous ammonia is also used legally by farmers, who fertilize their fields with it. Companies that make and sell anhydrous ammonia to farmers, then, are vulnerable; they may see their warehouses burglarized by meth lab cooks in search of the chemical. Additionally, the storage buildings at many farms have also been burglarized by drug makers in search of the ingredient.

Patty Taylor, the assistant manager of a fertilizer store in St. Jacob, Illinois, told the *Christian Science Monitor* in February 1999 that her store tried protecting its anhydrous ammonia supplies by padlocking and chaining its warehouse doors and by installing security lights. "It didn't make any difference," she said, adding that the store had been hit by thieves many times.

Walt Longo, a farm products supplier in Paloma, Illinois, was quoted in the same *Monitor* story. He told the newspaper that thieves tapped into one of his tanks of anhydrous ammonia, siphoned off a supply, but could not figure out how to shut off the tank. Instead, they left the valve open, spilling many gallons of the highly flammable compound on the floor of the warehouse. A hazardous materials team had to be called in to contain the spill. "Most of these guys are so desperate, they're willing to take any chances," Longo told the newspaper.

lies in rural Midwest towns and suburbs are also finding crystal meth affecting their communities, whether rich or poor.

One area of the community that is seriously affected by methamphetamine abuse is the workplace. In 2003, Quest Diagnostics, a firm that conducts some 7 million drug tests a year for employers, reported that meth use by workers and job applicants had increased by 68 percent over the prior year. Clearly, meth affects the way people perform their jobs. As a result, many people caught using meth by their employers face dismissal. For job applicants who test positive for meth, it is safe to say that not too many employers would want to take a chance on them. As more and more employers subject job applicants to drug testing, young people who use meth or other narcotics will find many doors closed to them as they try to begin careers.

Contaminated Homes and Cupcakes

It can cost several thousand dollars for a home or other building that once housed a meth lab to be cleaned of toxic chemicals and made habitable again. Typically, the carpets are ripped out and the walls and ceiling are scrubbed with alcohol and detergent. Because the toxic chemicals can be spread from room to room by the home's ventilation system, it is often recommended that the furnace and air conditioner, as well as all the home's ductwork, be ripped out and replaced. Because of the extensive work required, contractors can spend as much as three months on the cleanup of a former meth house.

Even though houses are cleaned, some state lawmakers believe prospective homeowners considering buying such a house have a right to know that it once contained a meth lab. Several states have adopted laws requiring real estate brokers to disclose that information to people considering buying such homes.

Concern over contamination from meth labs has affected other areas of daily life as well. In Iowa, for example, school board members in Mount Pleasant proposed a rule prohibiting students from bringing fresh-baked cupcakes and cookies to school, fearing that if those treats were baked in a home housing a meth lab, they could be contaminated with toxic chemicals. School board members worried that students would share the cakes with their classmates, exposing them to the harmful chemicals. The school board considered the ban because of the large number of meth labs that had been found in Mount Pleasant. Greg Lorber, an illegal drug specialist for the Iowa Department of Human Services, told the *Des Moines Register* in its February 18, 2005, issue, "It's a good precaution, considering what the situation is in that town."

Methamphetamine also causes problems outside of the workplace. Meth users often turn violent, even against their own families. In Contra Costa County, California, for example, police reported that nearly 90 percent of domestic violence calls were related to meth abuse. Frequently, communities where people manufacture or abuse methamphetamines have high crime rates. When there is a meth lab in the neighborhood, or drug deals occur on the streets, there is likely to be violence.

People who use meth cause other problems in their communities, often with horrible consequences, because the abusers lose touch with reality. In 2005, for instance, Scott Krause was arrested and charged with stealing a truck and crashing it head-on into a United Parcel Service van, killing the driver, Drew Reynolds. Krause had been a successful construction worker in California, earning $90,000 a year building high-priced homes, but when he fell into meth abuse, he started losing jobs and committing thefts to support his habit. On the day he stole the truck, Krause was allegedly high on meth and believed that monsters were chasing him.

The crime had a devastating impact on Lore Reynolds, who lost her husband in the accident, but also on the lives of the Krause family, who lost a husband and father to meth addiction and what may assuredly be a lengthy prison term. According to Krause's wife, Tracie, "There isn't a day that goes by that I don't think of Lore Reynolds and Drew."[38]

With her husband in jail, Tracie Krause had to find a way to support her family without his salary. Additionally, the Krauses endured embarrassment and shame in their tiny community in Nevada County, California. Eventually, the Krauses moved to the San Francisco area, where Tracie Krause found employment. "There was more than one incident," she said, "where my third- and fourth-grade children were told by friends . . . 'My parent said I can't play with you because of what your dad did.'" Tracie Krause said she hoped to start a new life away from Nevada County, where her children would not be constantly reminded of what happened when their father became addicted to methamphetamine. "Sometimes I remind them that once upon a time, Scott Krause was a kind, gentle, creative, capable, peaceful, devoted, loving family man, who worked hard to provide them a full and happy life."[39]

"The Emptiness at Home"

Drug-induced crimes can have a devastating impact on innocent victims. In September 2003, three young children were playing in the driveway of their home in Taylorsville, Utah, when an out-of-control car driven by Michael Joseph Whitton plowed into them. Two of the children—nine-year-old Jorge Robles-Ameda, and his sister, four-year-old Yanira Robles—were killed. The third child, six-year-old Christopher Robles, was severely injured but recovered. Still, his injuries required him to walk with leg braces, and he was expected to need surgery in the future to correct the damage to his body caused by Whitton's car.

Police learned that Whitton had consumed methamphetamine before getting into his car that day. Witnesses told police they saw Whitton's car race erratically before it shot over a curb and into the Robles' driveway. In May 2004, Whitton pleaded guilty to causing the deaths of the two children. He was sentenced to a jail term that could keep him locked up for as long as thirty years. "Of all the places in the community, a child should be safe in his or her own front yard," said Judge Pat Brian, who sentenced Whitton. "The defendant put in motion circumstances that were destined to result in tragedy and heartbreak sooner or later."[40]

During his tearful court appearance, Whitton faced Luis and Ana Saldana Robles, the parents of the dead children. "I wish I could take back that terrible accident," he told them. "If there was a way I could trade my life for those two young children, I would." Responded Luis Robles, "It is very painful to lose children. We feel the emptiness at home. The only child left behind will never be the same."[41]

Impaired Driving

People who ingest methamphetamine have no business getting behind the wheel of a car. In 2000, the U.S. National Highway Traffic Safety Administration examined issues surrounding drug abuse and driving at a conference in Seattle, Washington. The conference was composed of toxicologists—scientists who study the effect of chemicals and other substances on the human body and human performance. The toxicologists studied sixteen drugs, including some that are legally available as over-the-counter medications as well as others available only through prescriptions. Also, several illegal drugs, including methamphetamine, were studied. The toxicologists conducted the study to determine whether people under the influence of the different types of drugs

Although drugs and driving can be a deadly combination, studies have shown that some tractor-trailer drivers use methamphetamines to stay awake during long trips.

could safely operate motor vehicles. Among their conclusions was that meth users should not drive.

The agency issued a report stating that methamphetamine use "may impair the ability to engage in potentially hazardous activities such as driving a motor vehicle." It found that "Driving and driver behaviors included speeding, lane travel, erratic driving, accidents, nervousness, rapid and non-stop speech, unintelligible speech, disorientation, agitation, staggering and awkward movements, irrational and violent behavior, and unconsciousness. Impairment was attributed to distraction, disorientation, motor excitation, hyperactive reflexes, general cognitive impairment, or withdrawal, fatigue, and hypersomnolence [extreme sleepiness]."[42]

And yet, a shocking report issued in 2000 by the U.S. Substance Abuse and Mental Health Services Administration found that many interstate truck drivers admitted using methamphetamine to stay awake during long-distance runs. Interviewers spoke with truck drivers at roadside diners and truck stops between

Phoenix and Flagstaff in Arizona. Twenty truck drivers agreed to be interviewed over a three-day period in March 1998. According to the study, "Three of the 20 truck drivers interviewed had used methamphetamine. An additional nine said they knew another truck driver who used methamphetamine. . . . Of 20 drivers, 17 said that methamphetamine is easy to get. They reported that it is available in the back lots of most truck stops, easily obtained via CB radio contacts, and sold by both drivers and local dealers."[43]

The truck drivers said they are under considerable pressure to drive long distances in as little time as possible. As such, they find methamphetamine to be useful for remaining awake so they can spend more time on the road. The report pointed out that under

Drug Enforcement Agency (DEA) agents inspect chemicals from a meth lab in St. Louis. The chemicals used to manufacture the drug are exceedingly toxic.

federal law, interstate truck drivers are prohibited from spending more than ten hours a day behind the wheel of their rigs. And yet, the report stated, of the twenty drivers interviewed by SAMHSA, "only six drivers said they usually drive 10 hours in a 24-hour period. Three of the four who usually drive over 16 hours were stimulant [drug] users. Fourteen drivers admitted to violating the hours-of-service rules to some degree."[44] SAMHSA reported:

> Because of the sense of increased energy that methamphetamine supplies to users, it is often used in the workplace. Use by a truck driver who drives long distances for long hours on America's highways jeopardizes the safety of both the driver who uses and those who share the road. In a sample of fatally injured drivers, methamphetamine was found to be 7.3 percent. Some researchers say that these findings seem to "support a casual relationship between methamphetamine use and an increased risk of fatal accident involvement."[45]

Threat to the Environment

Perhaps the most substantial impact of meth on the community is what happens when police do uncover a drug lab operating in a neighborhood. Even if the neighborhood has been lucky and the lab has not exploded by the time police find it, there are still many serious problems that can be caused by the lab's existence. For instance, its impact on the environment can be extensive—streams in the vicinity may become polluted, noxious fumes may have been vented in the air, and even the lab's garbage sitting on the curb may be dangerous. As reported in the *Federal Bureau of Investigation Law Enforcement Bulletin*:

> Meth cooks sometimes use a formula for production that uses two extremely dangerous and highly volatile chemicals—sodium metal and anhydrous ammonia. Sodium metal can ignite when it comes into contact with water, and anhydrous ammonia is a deadly respiratory hazard. Some clan [clandestine] labs may even contain chemicals such as sodium cyanide, which, if accidentally mixed with another type of chemical found in the same lab, can produce a deadly hydrogen cyanide gas.[46]

According to the FBI, each pound of meth manufactured in a clandestine lab generates five pounds of toxic waste. The lab operators typically dump the waste in area streams or sewage systems,

Warnings to Hunters and Hikers

In fall of 2000, the Minnesota Department of Natural Resources warned hunters to "watch out for dangerous chemicals used by drug manufacturers in the making of methamphetamine." William Bernhjelm, the director of the agency's Enforcement Division, explained in a June 2001 edition of the *Rochester Post-Bulletin* that meth lab owners often dump dangerous waste chemicals in remote areas of state and county parks.

Meanwhile, 4-H clubs in Minnesota have been advised to be wary of the waste they find along roads and highways as they participate in anti-litter campaigns. The young 4-H members are told not to pick up plastic bottles that have tubes coming out of them and to not touch trash containing white powder or metal cylinders. Seventeen-year-old Katie Erickson, a 4-H club member, told the newspaper, "It is kind of frustrating that we're trying to do good for people and [that] there are people who can hurt people who are trying to help the community."

but often the toxicity of the waste remains in the neighborhood. In the home containing the lab, it is not unusual for the fumes to have penetrated walls, carpets, and ceilings.

In Rochester, Minnesota, Police Sergeant Dan Pulford is often called to inspect meth labs after the operators have been arrested. Wearing protective gear, Pulford said, he carefully inspects the contents of the homes. "There could be acid in a container that could kill you," he told a reporter. "Open it and it could blow up in your face."[47]

Of course, if the lab does explode, the dangers are magnified. For example, if a chemical fire breaks out in the neighborhood, the smoke may be poisonous, and the wind may carry it for miles. And, what is more, the firemen often do not know what they are dealing with when they arrive at the scene. When a chemical spill or fire erupts at a legitimate chemical company, the firemen are usually advised while they are en route to the scene about what type of substances to expect. Most states require chemical companies to make that information available in case of an emergency, so that fire authorities can take precautions and employ the proper equipment to fight the blaze. But when fire companies approach a meth lab that is on fire, they often have no way of knowing that they are facing more than just an ordinary house engulfed in flames.

Fire authorities near Millersport, Ohio, were fortunate when they arrived at the scene of a house fire. Alerted to the blaze by a witness, police and fire responders arrived to find two men inside the house trying to destroy items. Even though one of the men had been burned, neither man seemed to have much interest in leaving the dwelling even though it was still on fire. Police ordered the men outside and placed them under arrest.

Millersport Fire Captain Jerry Murphy said a brief inspection of the home's contents quickly told the true story: the home served as headquarters for a meth lab. Murphy said firemen discovered quantities of anhydrous hydroxide, ether, paint strippers, and other chemicals. He told a reporter, "We are trained to know what to look for. We just backed out and called for the HazMat (Hazardous Materials) teams."[48]

"Life After Meth"

People who are arrested for operating meth labs often face lengthy jail terms. Many meth users also end up in prison. Still, for many meth users, there is hope because of rehabilitation. Although it is clearly difficult to kick the meth habit, many users do find a way to shake their addictions and begin new lives. Indeed, there are many types of rehabilitation programs that help meth users regain control of their lives. In Craig, Colorado, for example, Kim Oliver used drugs, including meth, for twenty-two years but still found a way to kick her habit. She told a reporter, "I just want people to know there's life after meth."[49]

 **Chapter 4**

The Road to Recovery

More than 100,000 methamphetamine users a year enter rehabilitation programs, and stimulants—primarily methamphetamine—are one of five "major substances of abuse,"[50] according to the Substance Abuse and Mental Health Services Administration. (The other major substances of abuse are alcohol; opiates, primarily heroin; cocaine; and marijuana/hashish.) People who come to terms with their addictions and enter rehabilitation face a long and difficult struggle. Some meth users can kick their habits with outpatient treatment programs that last two or three months. Some crystal smokers need inpatient treatment; typically, they can expect to spend up to a month in such a program, where counselors watch over them twenty-four hours a day, seven days a week. But for many meth users, treatment begins in prison, where they find themselves spending lengthy terms of incarceration.

"Nothing Is Normal After Meth"

The U.S. Department of Justice says that 28 percent of all prisoners incarcerated in state institutions and 21 percent of inmates held in federal prisons have admitted to using methamphetamine or am-

Guards escort an inmate at a Texas prison. Studies indicate that more than 20 percent of prison inmates have used methamphetamines, and authorities believe that figure is rising.

phetamine in their lives. The statistics also show that meth use by lawbreakers is on the rise. The agency's Bureau of Justice Statistics reported that in 1989, just 2 percent of all inmates in U.S. jails reported using amphetamine or methamphetamine at the time they committed their crimes. Yet in 1996, the agency said, that figure jumped to 33 percent. Clearly, as methamphetamine comes to dominate the drug culture, more and more inmates are entering the nation's correctional system addicted to meth.

Twenty-seven-year-old Harry Meader is serving an eight-year term in a Minnesota prison for cooking and selling methamphetamine. Meader started abusing drugs at the age of thirteen, meaning he has spent nearly half his life ingesting illegal substances, including cocaine and heroin. At the age of nineteen, he had his first taste of meth. Soon after, he started cooking the drug on his own, first in the basement of a rural farmhouse and then in a rented auto body shop in the town of Austin. In 1999, police busted the lab in Austin and arrested Meader. After pleading guilty, he was sentenced to a lengthy prison term. "I'm glad I got caught," Meader told a reporter for the *Rochester Post-Bulletin*. "If I'd kept going the way I was going, I'd be dead."[51]

At one point during his meth abuse, Meader said, he had been awake for thirty-two straight days and weighed just one hundred and thirty-five pounds, some sixty-five pounds under his normal weight. He was also drinking heavily while abusing meth—as much as a bottle of whiskey in one sitting. Meanwhile, Meader said, his brain had virtually shut down. Normally a skilled auto mechanic, Meader said when he was abusing meth it would take him as long as four days to install a car stereo—a job that should take just a few hours.

Two years after entering prison, Meader was still battling his cravings for the drug. He said he found the cravings returning

---

Drug Hunger

Part of the difficulty in kicking the methamphetamine habit is due to a psychological condition known as "drug hunger." By using meth, users have inadvertently trained their brains to crave the drug in response to memories or emotions. Since the first hit of meth typically results in a feeling of euphoria, a similar feeling of euphoria could encourage users to want meth. In other words, since they remember that meth makes them happy, when the meth users are happy they crave the drug.

Minnesota psychiatrist Dr. Michael Palmen, in a June 28, 2001, interview with the *Rochester Post-Bulletin*, said, "After they're addicted to the drug, they'll have these natural experiences in life, which have to do with emotion, and they will trigger memories that then stimulate the part of their brain that is literally transformed into this addiction circuitry, which says, 'Once I feel this, I think this and then I have this urge harnessed to go get or take in or to do something to feel better.'"

Palmen said drug hunger can be triggered by something as simple as the words, "You want some?" Indeed, when meth users hear those words, they may be prompted to think they want the drug. "Once exposed to it," Palmen explained, "each person has a variable vulnerability to wanting to go back to using that drug again. That can be based on a person's initial response to the drug. If that's a really positive response in which they like the effect of the drug . . . then it is more likely they'll go back and try it again."

whenever he was reminded of meth—when he saw the powdered sugar atop a cupcake, heard song lyrics about drug abuse, or was confronted with any of a number of other reminders. To battle the cravings, Meader said, he tried to keep busy by reading and doing things with his hands. While in prison, Meader has developed his artistic talent and has even sold paintings to a Minnesota art gallery. "I'm doing something with my life," Meader told the newspaper. As for his lifetime addiction to meth, Meader said, "It ain't something you can do as a job. You can't function. Nothing is normal after meth. . . . Once you do meth, everything changes. It's got you."[52]

Drug Court

For people facing drug charges, there are alternatives to prison. Some communities have established "drug courts," which were established because of the recidivist nature of narcotics offenders—judges kept seeing the same defendants in court time after time. Obviously, the defendants were not receiving the drug rehabilitation they needed in jail, so after serving their sentences they would return to their drug dealing and drug abusing ways. The drug courts were set up as an alternative to the regular criminal justice system. When meth users are tried in drug court, the judge orders the defendants to enter a community-based rehabilitation program. During their time in the program—typically a year or more—they are required to undergo regular drug tests and report back to the judge at weekly or monthly intervals. If they complete the program and remain drug-free, prosecutors will drop the criminal charges against them.

Judge Barbara L. Brugnaux presides over one such county drug court in Vigo County, Indiana. Each day in her courtroom, she sees dozens of defendants who are required to report on their progress in staying drug free. As defendants talk about their successes, Brugnaux responds with words of encouragement. "Keep up the good work,"[53] she encourages one defendant.

Drug courts are not for everyone, however. Paul Southwick, coordinator of the drug court in Vigo County, told a reporter that

These former meth addicts lost custody of their children until they completed a drug treatment program that helped them kick their habit and build a steady home.

the success or failure of a drug rehabilitation program comes down to the desire of the participant to remain drug-free. In the seven years the Vigo County drug court has accepted defendants, Southwick said, nearly half of the participants tested positive for drug use while in rehab and were expelled from the drug court system, meaning they returned to the criminal justice system. "You can have the greatest treatment program," he remarked, "and, ultimately, it falls back on the individual's desire to change."[54]

Indeed, one woman called to appear before Brugnaux did not have positive results to report. Three weeks before this court appearance, the woman had tested positive for methamphetamine and the judge had ordered her to spend twenty-four hours in jail as a punishment. Since her release from jail, the woman's urine tests continued to show that she had been using meth. "What do you have to say for yourself?"[55] the judge asked the woman. The defendant gave the judge a tearful, inaudible reply. Brugnaux responded by sentencing the woman to more jail time. She was handcuffed, taken into custody in the courtroom, and led back to prison along with two men who also tested positive for meth.

Another long-time meth user appeared before Brugnaux that day. Crystal Helderman had started using meth at the age of thirteen; by the time she was eighteen, the drug had come to dominate her life. When she was arrested for theft at the age of eighteen, a judge told her she looked thirty. "Crystal, you've got problems," Vigo County Judge Michael H. Eldred had told her then. "Have you looked in the mirror recently?" Instead of going to jail, though, Helderman was permitted to enter the jurisdiction of Brugnaux's drug court. She spent three months at a residential treatment program, then spent more than a year attending counseling and group sessions and undergoing regular and random drug tests. Helderman told a reporter that Eldred's blunt remarks

The Best Drug Counselors

Sometimes the best drug counselors are former meth users who have dedicated their lives to helping make sure other young people do not make the same mistakes they did. In Edmonton, Canada, Corrine Grunsky spent four years on meth before freeing herself of her habit. Because of that experience, she started speaking at meetings of Narcotics Anonymous and Alcoholics Anonymous about addiction, and became active in a new Crystal Meth Anonymous group that started in her city.

"It's a young crowd that comes to the meetings—from 18 to 27—maybe, so that's good," Grunsky explained in the August 4, 2004, edition of the *Edmonton Examiner*. "Most of them are in treatment houses or living in straight houses." Grunsky said a support group might have helped her resist the drug when she was a teenager. "I worked hard to become a drug addict and get my dope," she remarked, "so it's going to be three times as hard getting back on to where I want to be. They [abusers] know they are in a trap when they are addicted. If they really want to quit, there's help out there."

Another former meth user who counsels others is Colorado resident Dena Harper, who spent nearly three decades as a meth addict before giving up the drug. She became a volunteer drug counselor so she could talk to young people about the dangers of crystal. She also started speaking with parents about what they can do to keep the drug away from children. "I've got mothers of kids who say, 'Dena, what can I do?'" Harper said in the May 25, 2004, issue of the *Craig Daily Press*. Harper said she tells them, "You've got to be tough with it. You need to talk to your kid and really listen to what they have to say."

woke her up. "I just looked sick," Helderman recalled. "To think the guys liked me. It was for my drugs. It certainly wasn't for my looks."[56]

Now twenty years old, Helderman stood before Brugnaux to report that she had completed her rehabilitation program and remained drug free. In return, Brugnaux issued the "graduate" a certificate of achievement for successfully kicking her meth addiction. "We have a lot to celebrate today,"[57] the judge said.

Making Good Decisions

For many meth users, entry into rehabilitation begins in a hospital emergency room. These users overdose and are rushed to the emergency room so physicians can work to stabilize their pulse, blood pressure, and body temperature, which can be affected by the drug. If the patient's body temperature is dangerously high,

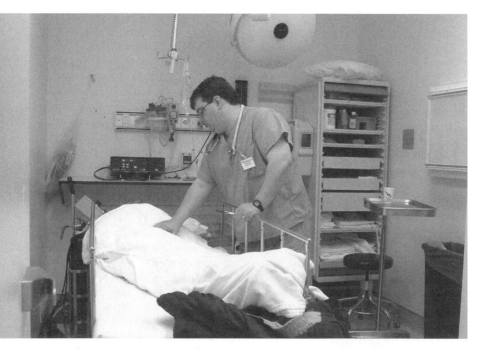

A doctor in Montana examines a man who has been brought to the hospital after overdosing on methamphetamine.

the physician may order an ice bath. Drugs may be prescribed to keep the patient from going into convulsions. Once the patient's vital signs have been stabilized, the physician may order the patient kept in a quiet environment for several hours or a day or more while the patient comes down from the high. Once the danger has passed, it is likely the patient will be urged to seek drug counseling and rehabilitation. If the police had been called to help transport the patient to the hospital, it is likely that drug possession charges will be filed; then a judge, either acting in drug court or presiding over a regular court, will order the person to enter rehabilitation.

For some substances of abuse, such as heroin and nicotine, other drugs can be substituted to wean users away from their addictions. That is not the case, however, with methamphetamine. Although antidepressants are occasionally prescribed to help meth users cope, generally there is no other way to give up crystal than to go cold turkey.

According to the National Institute on Drug Abuse, a meth recovery program should be designed to change a user's behavior pattern. The program should change the user's thinking about meth and also teach skills that help the user cope with problems and make the right decisions. "They have to hear the same things over and over again," said Mary Fulton, an Illinois drug counselor. "We have to be very patient with that person. It [meth use] can have some pretty serious physical and mental complications."[58]

Some meth users need only attend a program at an outpatient facility. Their addictions have not become so strong that they need constant monitoring of their activities in order to be rehabilitated. Typically, an outpatient program will require the drug user to attend a handful of sessions a week to meet with a counselor and participate in group discussions. During drug counseling, the counselor will help the client learn how to make good decisions, how to find ways to keep busy, and how to resist the cravings to use drugs. Meanwhile, the drug counselor will meet with the client's family to ensure that the user is receiving support at home. "A big part of it [rehabilitation] is trying to educate family and acquainting the patient with self-help groups, like Narcotics Anonymous," said Fulton. "This is a lifelong recovery, so it's very important to have support groups in place."[59]

The client will likely be urged to stay away from old friends who continue to abuse meth and other drugs. This is particularly important for young meth abusers, who must remain home with their parents and do not have the ability to move into new neighborhoods, find new jobs, and carve out new lives for themselves. "Many times they [addicts] must change their social environment," said Fulton. "They have to restructure their entire social surroundings."[60]

Like a Little Family

Of course, outpatient treatment programs do not work for everyone. Many meth users enter rehabilitation following long addictions and therefore require round-the-clock supervision. In those cases, the users must enter residential programs, which typically last from a month to six weeks.

Clients admitted to residential treatment facilities usually spend the first three to ten days in detoxification—a period in which the drug will be flushed from the body. Judy Morgan, a detoxification (or "detox") supervisor for the Illinois-based Vantage Point residential rehabilitation center, told a news reporter, "With meth, they are usually here [in detox] at least seven days. It seems like it takes longer for the mind to clear and the mental processes to start tracking well again. What we do is monitor them to make sure they remain stable and appear to get better instead of worse. . . . Part of it is just allowing them to rest and giving them a safe environment."[61]

Once they leave detox, the clients find their days structured from the moment they rise in the morning to lights-out at night. Morgan explains that it is important for recovering methamphetamine users to learn how to structure their lives—to become responsible for keeping appointments and for getting chores done on time and done well, for example. "Part of it [the recovery] is behavior modification," Morgan said. "They get up at a certain

A drug addict waits for counseling at the Addict Rehabilitation Center in New York. Such residential treatment centers help people to end their dependence on meth and other drugs.

time, go to bed at a certain time, are responsible for making their own bed. We reinstitute normal again."[62]

Many of the features of an outpatient program are instituted in a residential program as well. The client can expect to work with a counselor and attend group sessions where several former users talk about their experiences and the techniques that they rely on to maintain drug-free lives. "They become a little family in treatment because they are here for thirty days or longer," Morgan said. "They are learning how to change their social activities."[63]

After the drug user leaves treatment, whether it is an outpatient program or a residential facility, the rehabilitation still is not over. Clients leaving residential facilities may enter halfway houses before they return to living on their own. "There's always a step down or a step up after care,"[64] Morgan said, commenting on what happens after leaving a residential facility.

Group Therapy

A standard part of drug treatment is group therapy, in which clients who are taking part in treatment programs sit in a circle and discuss their addictions. Ron Miller, a former methamphetamine user who took part in a group session at an Illinois drug treatment center, talked to a reporter from the *Centralia Sentinel* about his experiences; his comments were published in its June 23, 2004 issue.

"The group meeting is 50 men from all over the state of Illinois sitting in chairs talking about their lives, their families, their stories," Miller said. "You can only imagine the types of conversation that transpire and the diverse background these people come from. [There are] guys as young as 18 to 73 all in the same meeting. The perspective they all have and the life experiences—it generates a tremendous amount of emotion and anxiety and learning how to deal with that anger and that guilt and not just storing all of those feelings and emotions inside anymore."

Each meeting starts with a "serenity prayer." The prayer reads: "God, give me the serenity to accept the things I cannot change." Members of the group then talk about how to face their problems rather than looking for ways to escape from them—such as through the use of drugs.

After leaving the rehabilitation program, Miller hoped to continue in group sessions by joining Narcotics Anonymous. Miller said it is important for former meth users to continue talking with others about the challenges they face. He explained that he plans to continue attending meetings to keep alive "that open, honest communication"; you need someone "to maintain that openness with," he said.

Female inmates take part in a group therapy session as part of a prison substance-abuse program.

Regardless of the treatment, most drug counselors remain in contact with the former users for months after they leave the programs. This contact does not ensure addicts will not use methamphetamine again. Indeed, most counselors expect their clients to give in to temptation and use drugs again, but because the contact with a counselor is maintained, former abusers have support. Also, since setbacks are expected, the counselors know how to react—how to convince the clients to return to drug-free lives. "We understand they may have slips,"[65] said Dawn Kleber, a substance abuse counselor at Vantage Point.

Do the Programs Work?

While many meth users who participate in outpatient or residential programs do kick their habits, there is also evidence that standard meth treatment programs can be improved. Crystal users, for example, have a high recidivism rate; after treatment, many of them return to using meth.

According to Wyoming psychologist Charles Bliss, one of the problems meth users encounter are the effects from brain cells that were damaged during their addictions. Studies have shown that the specific area of the brain affected by meth addiction controls motivation—the very trait meth users need to kick their habits. With their powers of motivation reduced by crystal abuse, Bliss said in an on-line essay, it is no wonder that meth users take much longer than other drug abusers to give up their addictions. He pointed out that many meth users return to the drug to avoid the depression they often feel as they rejoin society. "It therefore becomes difficult to remain drug-free when to do so means you will remain depressed for a very long time; 2-3 years with an average being about 2 years,"[66] Bliss wrote.

Bliss suggested that an effective residential program for methamphetamine users should span three to six months, and that an outpatient program should include four or five visits a week for up to a year. Following release from the program, the recovering meth user should meet with a counselor two or three times a week for the first year, Bliss advised, and once a week for the second year. He recommended that random drug testing should be a regular part of the recovering user's program. Wrote Bliss:

> Getting former methamphetamine users back to work as productive, contributing members of the community as soon as practical and sustainable for the patient is important for both the person in recovery from methamphetamine abuse and the community to which prior users often owe some restitution. However, aftercare support, extended beyond traditionally typical times, will be a critical treatment component supporting the methamphetamine user's recovery and decreasing chances that the person will again turn to methamphetamine and give up life as a productive, responsible, law-abiding citizen.[67]

Lives in Chaos

Not all meth users are ordered by courts to enter drug rehabilitation or are urged by emergency room physicians to seek treatment. In some cases, the meth users themselves finally come to the realization that they have to change their lives. Usually, they face the truth about themselves after hitting rock-bottom: they find themselves out of money and with no friends, with deteriorating health, and with lives that are in chaos. Maryann Jensen, a twice-divorced mother of two children, wrote that she started smoking crystal after meeting Roger, a new boyfriend who was addicted to the drug. At first, Jensen said, she was just a casual user, but soon her addiction to crystal grew. She said,

> I was inhaling crank a few times a day: before I went to work, around lunchtime (I'd make a quick dash home for my hits) and in the evening. The stuff was easy to buy if you had cash. One of Roger's friends had a sister who was a big dealer. For $25 you got enough powder to last a day and a half if you used it three times a day, doing two to three hits per time. That was a lot of money for me—my income was well under $30,000. But somehow I found a way to come up with the cash. Soon my credit cards were maxed out.[68]

Jensen was also losing weight; she had shed seventy-five pounds in just four months. She was not sleeping regularly and hardly ever ate. She stopped cleaning her house. She stole a co-worker's credit card and used it to draw out $600 in cash she needed to pay a drug dealer. "I had been sucked into a dangerous, self-destructive vortex," Jensen said, "but I couldn't see it at the time. And the physically exhausted, achy feeling I got as each high waned only made me long all the more for the next hit. Then I would feel good again—for awhile."[69]

At work, Jensen's supervisor finally confronted her and suggested that she needed to seek drug counseling. That night, Jensen decided to seek help. She described the experience:

> I checked into detox that night. I had a fever, and all of a sudden I realized I was totally run down—I hadn't eaten or slept well for nine months. The detox was a living hell. I felt absolutely crazy for the first three nights. But I hung in there, though I don't know how. Maybe it was the thought of my kids. . . . Throughout all this, there wasn't a day when I didn't crave the drug. Many times I thought, 'I'll do just one more hit.' But thanks to good therapy as well as emotional support from my kids and my older brother, Rick, I never did go back.[70]

Maryann Jensen completed a drug rehabilitation program and started to put her life back together. She took a second job to pay the debts accumulated during her addiction as well as the cost of her treatment. She also got rid of her boyfriend Roger. "I've learned a lot of lessons from this painful episode," she related, "but the most important one, I think, is that you can't expect someone else or something else, such as drugs, to provide your happiness. That emotion has to come from inside. And now, for the first time in my entire life, I know how it feels to be happy."[71]

Cracking Down

Harry Meader, Crystal Helderman, and Maryann Jensen took different paths to their meth addictions and different paths to emerge from their addictions. Clearly, though, the best way to avoid addiction is to resist the temptation to use drugs in the first place. Governments, social service agencies, and schools are working hard to send the message, particularly to young people, that methamphetamine is a dangerous drug. Meanwhile, police in the United States and Mexico are cracking down on meth labs, which are responsible for producing the drug that has become a major affliction for thousands of young Americans.

 **Chapter 5**

Fighting the War Against Methamphetamine

Methamphetamine abuse has exploded in the United States. While the drug is produced in illegal labs in basements, kitchens, and garages, a considerable supply is imported from Mexico and other countries. The federal government has responded by spending millions of dollars to investigate and prosecute drug kingpins. Also, lawmakers are clamping down on the availability of the chemicals needed to make the drug, particularly pseudoephedrine. Even with the crackdown, though, government officials and social workers believe the best way to keep methamphetamine out of the hands of young people is to educate them about the dangers of the drug.

Meth from Mexico

In the hills outside Hot Springs, Arkansas, police raided a home tucked far into the woods. Inside they found a meth lab operating right in the kitchen, while three young children sat at the kitchen table eating oatmeal. Following the bust, Drug Enforcement Administration spokesman Rusty Payne told a reporter, "Meth is now the No. 1 drug in rural America—absolutely, positively, end of question."[72]

There is no question that meth is a problem for police throughout the United States, but in recent times the drug has developed a wide following in rural areas of states like Arkansas, Tennessee, Missouri, and Iowa. Part of the reason for the rural meth epidemic is immigration: illegal Mexican laborers carrying meth find jobs on rural farms and then sell their drugs to local users. According to the U.S. National Drug Intelligence Center, a large proportion of meth is imported from Mexico and, to a lesser extent, from countries in Southeast Asia, such as Burma. According to the 2001 DEA report *Drug Trafficking in the United States*, "The entrée of ethnic Mexican traffickers into the methamphetamine trade in the mid-1990s resulted in a significant increase in the supply of the drug. Mexican criminal organizations, based in Mexico and California, provided high-purity, low-cost methamphetamine originally to cities in the Midwest and West with Mexican populations."[73]

As supplies of methamphetamine found their way from Mexico into California, they started making their way east. "This is a very real epidemic," Sheriff Ted Kamatchus of Marshall County, Iowa,

Agents with the Fresno, California, Methamphetamine Task Force search a camper while its resident, a farm worker from Mexico, sits handcuffed.

The Superlabs

Law enforcement authorities regard any meth lab that is capable of producing a ten-pound batch of the drug a "superlab." Ten pounds of meth in its crystal form translates to approximately forty-five hundred doses of the drug. In some cities, that quantity of meth can sell for more than $130,000 on the streets. Clearly, people who run superlabs make huge profits. Additionally, they and their labs impact the entire country. Drug agents say meth produced by the superlabs, most of which are believed to be in California, is sold not only by dealers in the West but by those in the Midwest and in cities on the East Coast.

In June 2000, drug agents busted a superlab near San Bernardino and confiscated four hundred pounds of meth. In 2001, police closed down nearly thirteen hundred meth labs in California, of which more than two hundred were superlabs. In 2003, police closed down a superlab in rural Glenn County, California, arresting eight people in an operation that allegedly brewed as much as seventy-five pounds of crystal meth at a time. Ed Pecis, a special agent for the California Bureau of Narcotics, told the *Sacramento Bee* newspaper in an October 17, 2004, interview that crystal produced at the lab was sold on the streets of Miami, Houston, and Los Angeles. The meth cooks thought they had a perfect, secluded location. "They were in a house on a hill, with a good line of sight and no law enforcement around," Pecis said. Obviously they had underestimated the agents who came to shut them down.

told a reporter. "Almost 80 percent of the drug cases we work on are methamphetamine cases, and we know the drugs are coming from Mexico. It is a problem that is tearing apart this community."[74] Kamatchus said he first realized that Mexican drug lords were in control of the meth trade in Marshall County when he heard about a meth user driving wildly through a cornfield, knocking down fence posts, because he thought Mexican drug gangs were trying to kill him.

Other small Midwest communities have found Mexican meth on their streets as well. In Duluth, Minnesota, police arrested two men in possession of two pounds of meth. Police believed the two men were couriers, transporting the meth to Minnesota from a drug lab in Mexico. "Methamphetamine is just an overwhelming problem in the state of Minnesota," Chief Roger Waller of the Duluth police said at a news conference. "More than 80 percent of methamphetamine coming into the state of Minnesota comes from Mexico."[75]

President George W. Bush's National Drug Control Strategy has identified meth as a primary drug threat. The strategy has three missions: to stop drug use before it starts, rehabilitate American drug users, and disrupt drug markets. In 2005, the Bush administration requested $66 million from Congress specifically to attack meth and similar drugs. The money was requested to create more than three hundred jobs for drug agents and federal prosecuting attorneys, who will be responsible for hunting down and prosecuting not only foreign drug kingpins doing business in the United States but local drug dealers as well.

Ephedrine from Canada

While law enforcement agencies explore ways to stem the flow of meth across the borders, they must also be concerned about the illegal importation of ephedrine and pseudoephedrine—the key ingredients of methamphetamine. The production of those chemicals is tightly controlled in the United States, but that is not the case in other countries. In testimony before a congressional

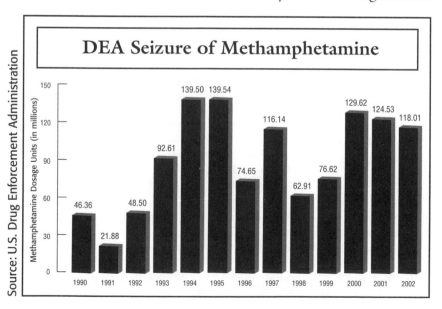

Source: U.S. Drug Enforcement Administration

committee in 2004, Scott Burns, a deputy director of the White House Office of National Drug Policy, said, "Most of the methamphetamine consumed in the United States is manufactured using diverted pseudoephedrine and ephedrine. . . . To counter the threat from methamphetamine, we and our neighbors, Mexico and Canada, must continue to tighten regulatory controls on pseudoephedrine and ephedrine, thousands of tons of which are smuggled illegally into the United States each year."[76]

Burns told members of Congress that Canadian authorities agreed to cooperate with U.S. drug agents to close down sources of pseudoephedrine and ephedrine. In September 2004, an investigation known as "Operation Brain Drain," conducted jointly by the DEA and the Royal Canadian Mounted Police, led to the breakup of a large Canadian-based meth ring that supplied not only the drug but its chemical components to labs in the United States. The investigation led to the arrests of 90 individuals and the seizure of 92 pounds of methamphetamine, 2,735 pounds of

Meth and Identity Theft

Many meth labs are busted by police investigating cases of identity theft, a crime in which a thief uses an innocent person's credit card numbers to draw money or buy goods on credit in the victim's name. Identity theft is often perpetrated by people who steal mail or sift through trash cans in search of credit card receipts and statements.

Police have found that meth addicts and cooks need a steady source of money, so they often resort to identity theft. When police trace credit card purchases to delivery addresses, they often find meth labs operating in the homes. In 2005, for example, a judge in Eugene, Oregon, sentenced meth addict Shay Kale Prim to fifteen years in prison after the man was convicted of forty-five counts of identity theft. When he was arrested, Prim was found in possession of credit card numbers and pieces of identification belonging to some seventy people.

As many as 95 percent of identity theft crimes are committed by people to support a meth habit or to raise money to buy chemicals for their meth labs, Tom Montgomery of the Seattle office of the U.S. Postal Inspection Service, told the *Seattle Post-Intelligencer* for a story in its July 23, 2001, issue. "Almost without exception, the people we're arresting for these types of crimes are doing meth," he said. "It's a plague."

ephedrine powder, some 1.7 million ephedrine pills, 62 pounds of assorted other chemicals used to make meth, 5 gallons of liquid meth, and 2 kilograms of cocaine.

According to authorities, the ring not only sold meth and ephedrine to American buyers but shipped the chemicals to Mexico to supply labs based in that country. Those labs, in turn, sold the drugs in the United States. Deputy DEA Administrator Michele Leonhart said, "This should send a clear message to those who manufacture and traffic illegal drugs that you could be next. Thanks to the cooperative success of this investigation between the two countries, we have identified the most significant sources of ephedrine from Canada to the United States. Breaking up these organizations will dramatically limit the availability of ephedrine in the United States and will have a significant effect on the large scale production of methamphetamine in the United States."[77]

Widespread Crackdown

The federal government has committed other resources to the meth epidemic. For example, the U.S. Justice Department's Organized Crime Drug Enforcement Task Force operates under a $500 million budget per year. In 2003, the Task Force—which is composed of police from several federal, state, and local law enforcement agencies—broke up 142 meth rings. Indeed, meth cases account for 26 percent of the Task Force's investigations.

These efforts were partly the result of an effort made by the DEA to learn about the extent of the meth problem and what it would take to stamp out the drug. In 2002, then–DEA Director Asa Hutchinson conducted the "Meth in America: Not in Our Town" program. Hutchinson visited thirty-two states to listen to local police officials tell him what they needed to combat the illegal meth business in their communities.

Still, methamphetamine continues to find its way into American communities. During the early 21st century, meth started moving east from the West Coast and Midwest farm fields onto the streets of the large eastern cities. Early in 2005, for example, police raided the basement of a row house in Philadelphia, where they found thirty-seven pounds of crystal meth with a street value of $1.7 million. Asked to comment on the bust, DEA agent David Taylor told a Philadelphia newspaper, "You Northeasterners are the last bastion that hasn't been hit yet. But I hate to tell you: It's coming."[78]

Penalties for Traffickers

Lab operators, dealers, and others in the crystal meth business face stiff penalties if convicted of selling the drug. The 1970 U.S. Controlled Substances Act established penalties that include heavy fines and imprisonment for illegal use or sale of drugs. In addition, the 1986 U.S. Anti-Drug Act established mandatory minimum sentences for people convicted of selling meth and other drugs. Under the law, a meth dealer convicted of a first offense must go to prison for a term of not less than five years, although depending on the quantity of the drug and whether violence is involved in the operation, the dealer could receive as much as forty years in prison. A second conviction for selling methamphetamine includes a mandatory sentence of at least ten years and a possible sentence of as long as life behind bars. Those penalties apply only to meth dealers prosecuted in the federal courts. Meth dealers prosecuted in the state courts face penalties established by state legislatures, but most of those have followed the lead of the Controlled Substances Act and enacted harsh and lengthy penalties on drug dealers as well.

Even though the penalties are harsh, the profit potential in the meth business is large enough for people to take the risk of getting involved. One such individual is the local "meth king" in Jackson County, Missouri, whom police identified as Michael Wayne Duncan, a man alleged to have made huge profits cooking and selling meth over a period of several years. "Duncan was seen as almost a sort of guru," federal prosecutor Mark Miller told a reporter. "People looked up to him in a way that was almost religious because of his ability to cook."[79]

With profits from the meth business, Duncan was able to buy luxury homes, boats, island homes, and gold jewelry, and, when

Federal Trafficking Penalties for Methamphetamines (Schedule II)

Quantity	Penalties
10 to 99 gms pure or 100 to 999 gms mixture	**First offense:** Not less than 5 years and not more than 40 years. If death or serious injury, not less than 20 or more than life. Fine of not more than $2 million if an individual, $5 million if not an individual.
	Second offense: Not less than 10 years, and not more than life. If death or serious injury, life imprisonment. Fine of not more than $4 million if an individual, $10 million if not an individual.

Quantity	Penalties
100 gm or more pure or 1 kg or more mixture	**First offense:** Not less than 10 years, and not more than life. If death or serious injury, not less than 20 or more than life. Fine of not more than $4 million if an individual, $10 million if not an individual.
	Second offense: Not less than 20 years, and not more than life. If death or serious injury, life imprisonment. Fine of not more than $8 million if an individual, $20 million if not an individual.
	2 or more offenses: Life imprisonment.

he was finally arrested, he had enough cash available to post bail of nearly $3 million. Out on bail, he continued to cook meth and was severely burned when his lab exploded. After recovering from his burns, Duncan was tried, convicted, and sentenced to nineteen years in a federal prison. In sentencing Duncan, U.S. District Judge Fernando J. Gaitan Jr., rebuked him, "You are a link in the chain which chokes the lifeblood from our communities."[80]

Restrictions on Pseudoephedrine Products

Meanwhile, state legislatures have taken action to attack the meth trade. By 2005, for instance, many state governments in the United States had passed or proposed a variety of measures to restrict the sale of pseudoephedrine. In Oklahoma, manufacturers and wholesalers are required to keep records of who buys large quantities of the drug. In Oregon and Illinois, cold remedies containing pseudoephedrine can be sold in pharmacies only and must

---

How to Bust a Meth Lab

Police preparing to bust down the door of a meth lab take along their badges and guns, but their equipment also includes respirators, rubber-coated gloves, and fire- and chemical-resistant suits. In fact, federal regulations mandate that all police officers who participate in meth lab busts undergo at least twenty-four hours of training in the handling of hazardous chemicals.

For police officers who wish to specialize in meth lab investigations, the U.S. Drug Enforcement Administration conducts week-long schools at training sites in Quantico, Virginia, and Overland Park, Kansas. Local police officers are taught how to raid and dismantle labs.

In their training, police are told never to smoke near a suspected meth lab and not to touch, taste, or smell the equipment they find inside. They are advised to avoid touching light switches; even the tiniest electrical spark created by a switch turning on or off can ignite fumes in the room. Likewise, they are told not to plug in or unplug electrical devices. Following the bust, police are advised to clean and decontaminate their tools and clothes.

Contamination from meth labs is such a problem that when police officers go to make arrests at meth labs, many bring along a change of clothes for the people they arrest because their clothes may be contaminated. Police do not even want the contaminated clothes to come into contact with the upholstery in their squad cars.

Even prison workers have to be careful. At the Olmsted County prison in Minnesota, the clothes from a meth lab worker were placed in a plastic bag. Soon, prison authorities discovered that holes had formed in the bag—the chemicals in the clothes were eating through the plastic. "The guys getting arrested at the lab scenes are a walking waste dump," Steve Von Wald, director of the Olmsted County jail, told the *Rochester Post-Bulletin* in a June 25, 2001, interview.

be kept behind the counter; they are no longer available on the shelves of supermarkets and convenience stores. In Tennessee, legislators adopted a similar law in 2005. The measure was introduced in the Tennessee legislature after police arrested a man hired by meth cooks to buy or steal boxes of cold medicine from retail stores. "He basically was paid by meth cooks in middle Tennessee to either steal or buy as much ephedra as he could," said Knoxville police spokesman Ed Kingsbury. "Every 10 boxes, he would get paid $100, or a gram of dope."[81]

On the federal level, in 2005 Congress began considering a bill that would restrict sales of cold medicine containing pseudoephedrine. "The most effective thing we can do to make meth harder to manufacture is to put cold medicine behind the counter at pharmacies and require purchasers to sign for it and show a photo ID,"[82] said U.S. Senator Dianne Feinstein of California, a co-sponsor of the bill.

Smurfing and Shelf Sweeping

These efforts by the state and federal lawmakers are also designed to crack down on the practices known as "smurfing" and "shelf sweeping." Smurfing occurs when a drug ring sends a large number of individuals—all likely to be meth users themselves—into a store or group of stores in a specific neighborhood to buy individual boxes of cold remedies. Shelf sweeping occurs when a group of meth users suddenly enters a store and rushes to the cold remedy aisle, where the users grab as many boxes of cold medicine as they can, then rush out to waiting get-away cars. The practice is similar to the smash-and-grab style of theft, in which a burglar breaks a store window and then grabs jewelry or other expensive items on display.

Some large retailers have taken their own action, rather than relying only on federal or state legislation. Wal-Mart and Costco as well as the Rite-Aid and Walgreens pharmacy chains have already instructed their pharmacists to keep cold remedies containing pseudoephedrine behind the counters or to otherwise limit sales of the medications to customers.

A sign at a store in Iowa directs customers to the pharmacy counter, as part of an effort to control the sale of methamphetamine ingredients like pseudoephedrine.

Lawmakers also have considered other measures involving meth labs. Specifically, some of the laws are designed to protect children living in homes where meth is made. Under statutes that have been adopted in Alaska, Arizona, Colorado, Iowa, Minnesota, Montana, North Dakota, Utah, and Washington, those children can be taken from their parents and placed in protective homes. Similarly, on a national level, the White House Office of National Drug Control Policy has established the Drug Endangered Children Program to help police and social workers provide medical attention and find temporary shelter for children found sharing their homes with meth labs. According to the agency, some three thousand children were living in homes with meth labs in 2002, and it is likely that about thirteen hundred suffered from exposure to the toxic chemicals. What is more, when parents are cooking and/or using meth, it is likely they are neglecting their children. "Parents will go on a meth binge for three days, then crash for 48 hours, and during that time no one is watching the kids,"[83] according to Scott Burns, a deputy director for the control policy office.

Learning About the Dangers

If young people learn about the dangers of meth through their schools, the media, or through the work of community organizations, there is a chance they will never try the drug. With that goal in mind, a number of organizations have launched education programs throughout the United States to deliver the message that meth is bad for young people.

For example, in 2004 the Partnership for a Drug-Free America started running public service announcements warning parents and teenagers about the dangers of meth. Funded by American corporations and media organizations that provide free advertising space, the Partnership runs print ads and airs television and radio commercials aimed at convincing young people to stay away from drugs. The meth-related print ads were aimed at parents. They depicted a number of teenagers complaining about having nothing to do, finally disclosing that the teenagers who complain most about boredom are the ones most likely to try meth. The meaning is clear: Parents would do well to listen to the messages their teenagers are sending.

In the United States today, there are dozens of highly effective drug prevention programs established by schools and local groups as well as national organizations. They are targeted at children of all ages, from the pre-school level through high school. Many of the programs send straightforward messages about drug abuse. Some try to reach out directly to teen drug users or teens at risk. Sometimes, these programs do not provide a specific anti-drug message; rather, they try to provide young people with the cognitive skills that help them make their own decisions about whether to use drugs. In a 1991 National Institute on Drug Abuse report on the growth of methamphetamine in the United States, James N. Hall, the executive director of the Up Front Drug Information Center in Florida, and Pauline M. Broderick, the center's director of research, said:

> Community-based networks are a vital resource for countering the problems of alcohol and other drug abuse. Indeed, such organizations represent the "homefront" of the "war on drugs." The impact of these networks is particularly appropriate for addressing the spread of domestically produced methamphetamine. . . . The localized nature of methamphetamine epidemics emphasizes the need for creative prevention strategies created by community-based networks. Such groups are in the best position to determine the most appropriate way of marketing and disseminating drug prevention messages.[84]

One such community-based prevention program can be found in Terre Haute, Indiana, where Chuck Tharp and Mike Eslinger, Indiana state troopers, visit schools to explain how meth labs operate and what makes them so dangerous. Tharp and Eslinger take along a box of cold pills, a fire extinguisher, some camera batteries, a package of coffee filters, a plastic funnel, and various chemicals, including acetone and rubbing alcohol. "What you're looking at is one complete meth lab,"[85] Tharp told the students at Sullivan High School during a program in the school's cafeteria.

Eslinger, meanwhile, told the students to be wary of tweakers—people using meth. "These people don't care about anything but their dope," Eslinger told the young people. "Don't try to be a hero. Be very, very careful with these people."[86]

Elsewhere in the Terre Haute area, educators, police officers, business executives, and drug counselors established the Coalition Against Methamphetamine Abuse. In its first year of existence, the coalition presented ten programs, about the dangers of meth use, to businesses, church groups, physicians, and hospital staff members. Kristin Chittick, a founder of the coalition, told a news reporter that the group was founded to keep meth out of the region. "This community is not going to tolerate this," she said.[87]

Meanwhile, the rise in crystal addiction in the homosexual community has prompted many gay activists to launch a crusade

Gay Pride 2004

Another night on the A list? If the weekend comes and you never leave your apartment, maybe you haven't heard. HIV infection rates are on the rise again, syphilis is up 1200 percent in just four years, and there's an epidemic of crystal meth use. It's very popular this year... but that one you probably knew.

CRYSTAL METH: NOTHING TO BE PROUD OF

CRYSTAL METH WORKING GROUP–HIV FORUM WWW.HIVFORUMNYC.ORG

In recent years, groups like HIV Forum NYC have distributed public service announcements like this one, warning young gays about the dangerous consequences of using crystal meth.

against meth abuse as well. Since crystal can be liquefied and injected through a needle—a process by which AIDS is often transmitted—the meth epidemic in the gay community has led to renewed fears of the spread of AIDS. One gay rights group, the HIV Forum NYC, has launched an advertising campaign in New York aimed at gay crystal meth users. Another group, the Gay Men's Health Crisis, operates a hotline that fields calls from gay men concerned about crystal meth use. "Thank god for the GMHC and the HIV Forum," said John Blair, a New York City bar owner who is gay. "In the last year, things have started to turn around. Using crystal is not something you brag about anymore. There's a growing stigma against it, especially among the younger set. As people get more and more information, they realize the harm it's doing, not just to users but to the community as a whole."[88]

There is no question that efforts by groups as diverse as Terre Haute's Coalition Against Methamphetamine Abuse and New York's HIV Forum are helping to keep meth out of the hands of many. Ultimately, though, it is up to young people to realize that experimenting with a bowl of crystal meth can lead to devastating consequences that can include severe health problems, mental illness, imprisonment, and a lifetime battling addiction against what has proven to be a truly monstrous drug.

Notes

Introduction: "The Ugliest Drug There Is"

1. U.S. Department of Justice, *Final Report of the Methamphetamine Interagency Task Force*, 1999. www.ojp.usdoj.gov/nij/methintf/b.html.
2. Quoted in Matt Bai, "White Storm Warning," *Newsweek*, March 31, 1997, p. 67.
3. Quoted in Andrew Ross, "The New Suburban High," *Good Housekeeping*, September 1999, p. 89.
4. Quoted in "Dying for Crystal," *People*, February 16, 2004, p. 95.
5. Quoted in Walter Kirn, "Crank," *Time*, June 22, 1998, p. 29.

Chapter 1: Speed Kills

6. Quoted in Edward M. Brecher, "The Consumers Union Report on Illicit and Licit Drugs," *Consumer Reports Magazine*, 1972. www.druglibrary.org/schaffer/Library/studies/cu/CU37.html.
7. Quoted in Brecher, "The Consumers Union Report on Illicit and Licit Drugs."
8. Pennsylvania Crime Commission, *Organized Crime in Pennsylvania: A Decade of Change*,1990, p. 201.
9. Quoted in Anthony R. Lovett, "Wired in California," *Rolling Stone*, May 5, 1994, p. 39.
10. Quoted in Paul Solotaroff, "A Plague in the Heartland," *Rolling Stone*, January 23, 2003, p. 49.
11. Quoted in Amy Hatten, "Meth Use Growing Among Teens," *Craig Daily Press*, May 18, 2004. www.craigdailypress.com/section/darkcrystal/storypr/12081.
12. *Pulse Check: National Trends in Drug Abuse*. www.white-

housedrugpolicy.gov/publications/drugfact/pulsechk/jan uary04/.

13. Quoted in Ross, "The New Suburban High."

14. Quoted in Hatten, "Meth Use Growing Among Teens."

Chapter 2: The Physical Effects of Methamphetamine

15. Quoted in Brecher, "The Consumers Union Report on Illicit and Licit Drugs."

16. Quoted in Brecher, "The Consumers Union Report on Illicit and Licit Drugs."

17. Quoted in Jeremy Browning, "I Was in a Bad, Bad Way," *Craig Daily Press*, May 11, 2004. www.craigdailypress.com /section/darkcrystal/storypr/11980.

18. Quoted in Per Ola and Emily D'Aulaire, "A Dangerous Drug Hits the Heartland," *Reader's Digest*, April 1999, p. 141–42.

19. Quoted in Betty Ann Bowser, "Drug Trends," *PBS News hour*, December 10, 1997. www.pbs.org/newshour/bb/ health/july-dec97/meth_12-10.html.

20. Quoted in Brecher, "The Consumers Union Report on Licit and Illicit Drugs."

21. Quoted in Browning, "I Was in a Bad, Bad Way."

22. U.S. Centers for Disease and Control and Prevention, *Morbidity and Mortality Weekly Report*, June 1, 2001, pp. 433–34. www.cdc.gov/mmwr/

23. Quoted in Miriam Hill, "Drug Seduces Many to Reckless Behavior," *Philadelphia Inquirer*, February 15, 2005, p. A-8.

24. Quoted in Hill, "Drug Seduces Many to Reckless Behavior," p. A-8.

25. Quoted in Karen Karbashewski, "Crystal Meth Takes Terrible Toll on Mind and Body," *Edmonton Examiner*, August 11, 2004. www.edmontonexaminer.com/pages /newsroom/meth_3.html.

26. Quoted in Karin Grunden, "Nearly Fatal Attraction:

Young Mother's Addiction Proves Costly," *Terre Haute Tribune-Star*, January 21, 2003. www.tribstar.com/articles/2003/01/21/news/export34200.prt.

27. Quoted in Grunden, "Nearly Fatal Attraction: Young Mother's Addiction Proves Costly."

28. Quoted in Dawn Schuett, "Meth's Toll on Children Still Being Evaluated," *Rochester Post Bulletin*, June 27, 2001. www.postbulletin.com/meth/stories/day4/65414.shtml.

29. Quoted in Schuett, "Meth's Toll on Children Still Being Evaluated."

30. Quoted in Browning, "I Was in a Bad, Bad Way."

31. Quoted in Tom Gorman, "Witness to Fire Says Men Didn't Try to Save Children," *Los Angeles Times*, December 28, 1998, p. A-1.

32. Quoted in Anastasia Toufexis, "There Is No Safe Speed," *Time*, January 8, 1996, p. 37.

Chapter 3: The Effect of Methamphetamine on Society

33. Quoted in Cynthia Hanson, "I Had No Idea My Child Was on Drugs," *Ladies Home Journal*, March 1997, p. 68.

34. Quoted in Hanson, "I Had No Idea My Child Was on Drugs," p. 68.

35. Quoted in Hanson, "I Had No Idea My Child Was on Drugs," p. 66.

36. Quoted in "Young Couple on Meth Die in Nebraska Snowstorm," The Associated Press, Saturday, January 22, 2005. http://www.foxnews.com/story/0,2933,145128,00.html

37. Quoted in Amy Olson, "A Family Struggles with Meth," *Rochester Post-Bulletin*, June 23, 2001. www.postbulletin.com/meth/stories/day1/64945.shtml.

38. Quoted in Roman Gokhman, "Tough Year for Suspect's Family," *Grass Valley Union*, January 6, 2005. www.theunion.com/article/20050106/NEWS/101060061/-1/THEMES02.

39. Quoted in Gokhman, "Tough Year for Suspect's Family."
40. Quoted in Linda Thomson, "Driver Sentenced in Killing of 2," *Deseret Morning News*, March 12, 2004. http://deseretnews.com/dn/print/1,1442,59504530,00.html.
41. Quoted in Thomson, "Driver Sentenced in Killing of 2."
42. National Highway Traffic Safety Administration. *Drug and Human Performance Fact Sheets.* www.nhtsa.dot.gov/people/injury/research/job185drugs/methamphetamine.htm.
43. U.S. Department of Health and Human Services. *Communication Strategy Guide: A Look at Methamphetamine Use Among Three Populations.* http://media.shs.net/prevline/pdfs/index.pdf.
44. U.S. Department of Health and Human Services. *Communication Strategy Guide: A Look at Methamphetamine Use Among Three Populations.*
45. U.S. Department of Health and Human Services. *Communication Strategy Guide: A Look at Methamphetamine Use Among Three Populations.*
46. Guy Hargreaves, "Clandestine Drug Labs," *FBI Law Enforcement Bulletin*, vol. 69, no. 4, April 2000, pp. 3–4.
47. Quoted in Janice Gregorson, "Any Can, Any House Is a Risky Unknown," *Rochester Post-Bulletin*, June 25, 2001. www,postbulletin.com/meth/stories/day2/65109.shtml.
48. Quoted in Carl Burnett Jr., "Meth Lab Found in Millersport," *Lancaster Eagle-Gazette*, February 16, 2005. www.lancastereaglegazette.com/news/stories/20050216/localnews/1995214.html.
49. Quoted in Christina M. Currie, "Breaking the Cycle," *Craig Daily Press*, June 1, 2004. www.craigdailypress.com/section/darkcrystal/storypr/12255.

Chapter 4: The Road to Recovery

50. U.S. Substance Abuse and Mental Health Services Administration, *Treatment Episode Data Set Highlights*, 2002.

wwwdasis.samhsa.gov/teds02/2002_teds_highlights.pdf.

51. Quoted in Amy Olson, "Prison Was the Best Thing to Happen," *Rochester Post-Bulletin*, June 23, 2001. www.postbulletin.com/meth/stories/day1/64939.shtml.

52. Quoted in Olson, "Prison was the Best Thing to Happen."

53. Quoted in Karin Grunden, "Judge Believes Drug Court Offers Solution," *Terre Haute Tribune-Star*, January 24, 2003. www.tribstar.com/articles/2003/01/24/news/export34406.prt.

54. Quoted in Grunden, "Judge Believes Drug Court Offers Solution."

55. Quoted in Grunden, "Judge Believes Drug Court Offers Solution."

56. Quoted in Karin Grunden, "Mother Walks Long, Hard Path to Rehabilitation," *Terre Haute Tribune-Star*, January 23, 2003. www.tribstar.com/articles/2003/01/23/news/export34349.prt.

57. Quoted in Grunden, "Judge Believes Drug Court Offers Solution."

58. Quoted in Ashley Wiehlc, "Relapse Not Uncommon on Road to Meth Recovery," *Centralia Morning Sentinel*, June 20, 2004. www.morningsentinel.com.

59. Quoted in Wiehle, "Relapse Not Uncommon on Road to Meth Recovery."

60. Quoted in Wiehle, "Relapse Not Uncommon on Road to Meth Recovery."

61. Quoted in Ashley Wiehle, "Meth Rehab Centers Provide Round-the-Clock Treatment," *Centralia Morning Sentinel*, June 22, 2004. http://www.morningsentinel.com/News/2004/0622/Front_Page/087.html.

62. Quoted in Wiehle, "Meth Rehab Centers Provide Round-the-Clock Treatment."

63. Quoted in Wiehle, "Meth Rehab Centers Provide Round-the-Clock Treatment."

64. Quoted in Wiehle, "Meth Rehab Centers Provide Round-the-Clock Treatment."

65. Quoted in Wiehle, "Meth Rehab Centers Provide Round-the-Clock Treatment."
66. Charles Bliss, "Methamphetamine: How Effective Are Current Treatment Programs?" www.cornerstonebh.com/meth4.htm
67. Bliss, "Methamphetamine: How Effective Are Current Treatment Programs?"
68. Maryann Jensen, "I Got Hooked on Drugs," *McCall's*, February 1997, p. 51.
69. Jensen, "I Got Hooked on Drugs," p. 51.
70. Jensen, "I Got Hooked on Drugs," p. 56.
71. Jensen, "I Got Hooked on Drugs," p. 57.

Chapter 5: Fighting the War Against Methamphetamine

72. Quoted in Dirk Johnson, "Policing a Rural Plague," *Newsweek*, March 8, 2004, p. 41.
73. U.S. Department of Justice, *Drug Trafficking in the United States*. www.usdoj.gov/dea/concern/drug_trafficking.html
74. Quoted in Dan McGraw, "The Iowan Connection: Powerful Mexican Drug Cartels Have Hit Rural America," *U.S. News and World Report*, March 2, 1998, p. 34.
75. Quoted in Mark Stodghill, "Police Seize Two Pounds of Meth," *Duluth News Tribune*, January 12, 2005. www.duluthsuperior.com/mld/duluthsuperior/news/local/10624808.htm.
76. Testimony of Scott Burns, U.S. Drug Enforcement Administration, before the House Committee on Government Reform, February 6, 2004. http://reform.house.gov/Uploaded Files/Burns.pdf.
77. Drug Enforcement Agency (news release), "DEA Eliminates Major Source of U.S. Meth." www.usdoj.gov/dea/pubs/pressrel/pr092304.html.
78. Quoted in Alfred Lubrano, "Police Try to Get a Jump on

Meth," *Philadelphia Inquirer*, February 14, 2005, p. A-1.

79. Quoted in Peter Wilkerson, "America's Drug: Postcards from Tweakville," *Rolling Stone*, February 19, 1998, p. 53.

80. Quoted in Wilkerson, "America's Drug: Postcards from Tweakville," p. 53.

81. Quoted in Catharyn Campbell, "Investigators, Pharmacists Support Governor's Anti-Meth Package." www.wate.com /global/story.asp?s=2880682&ClientType.

82. Quoted in Ruby Gonzales, "Bill Would Require ID to Buy Some Cold Medications," *Los Angeles Daily News*, February 13, 2005. www.dailynews.com/Stories/0,1413, 200%7E20954%7E2708763,00.html.

83. Quoted in George Gannon, "Police, Social Workers say Meth Labs Pose Great Risk to Children," *Charleston Daily Mail*, January 10, 2005, p. 1-A. www.dailymail.com/news/News /2005011020/display_story.php?sid=2005011020&f

84. James N. Hall and Pauline M. Broderick, "Community Networks for Response to Abuse Outbreaks of Methamphetamine and Its Analogs," *Methamphetamine Abuse: Epidemiologic Issues and Implications* (Research Monograph 115). Rockville, Md.: National Institute on Drug Abuse, 1991, pp. 109, 117.

85. Quoted in Karin Grunden, "Education Key to Slowing Epidemic," *Terre Haute Tribune-Star*, January 25, 2003. www.tribstar.com/articles/2003/01/26/news/export34 470.prt.

86. Quoted in Grunden, "Education Key to Slowing Epidemic."

87. Quoted in Grunden, "Education Key to Slowing Epidemic."

88. Quoted in Frank Owen, "No Man Is a Crystal Meth User Unto Himself," *New York Times*, August 29, 2004. www.nytimes.com/2004/08/29/fashion/29METH.html.

Organizations to Contact

Crystal Meth Anonymous
8205 Santa Monica Boulevard
West Hollywood, CA 90046-5977
(213) 488-4455
www.crystalmeth.org

The national organization coordinates chapters in more than fifty cities in the United States and Canada, where recovering meth users meet regularly to help one another stay clean. The organization's website provides links to the local chapters.

Drug Enforcement Administration
2401 Jefferson Davis Highway
Alexandria, VA 22301
(202) 307-1000
www.usdoj.gov/dea

The U.S. Justice Department's chief anti-drug law enforcement agency is charged with investigating the illegal narcotics trade in the United States and helping local police agencies with their anti-drug efforts. Young visitors to the agency's website can find the agency's book *Get It Straight* available on-line, which features a section titled "What's Up With Methamphetamine?"

Narcotics Anonymous
PO Box 9999
Van Nuys, CA 91409

(818) 773-9999

www.na.org

Narcotics Anonymous supports thousands of weekly meetings which serve as forums for members to help one another emerge from their addictions.

National Drug Intelligence Center

319 Washington Street, 5th Floor

Johnstown, PA 15901-1622

(814) 532-4601

www.usdoj.gov/ndic

Also part of the Justice Department, the agency provides intelligence on drug trends to government leaders and law enforcement agencies. The agency's intelligence brief, *Children at Risk*, can be downloaded at the center's Website.

National Institute on Drug Abuse

6001 Executive Boulevard, Room 5213

Bethesda, MD 20892-9561

(301) 443-1124

www.nida.nih.gov

Part of the National Institutes of Health, the NIDA's mission is to help finance scientific research projects that study addiction trends and treatment of chronic drug users. The University of Michigan's 2004 *Monitoring the Future* report can be accessed through the NIDA website.

Partnership for a Drug-Free America

405 Lexington Avenue, Suite 1601

New York, NY 10174

(212) 922-1560.

www.drugfreeamerica.org

Funded by American corporations and media organizations that provide free advertising space, the Partnership helps convince young people to stay away from drugs. On the organization's

website, many former methamphetamine users and their family
members have posted personal messages.

Substance Abuse and Mental Health Services Administration
1 Choke Cherry Road
Room 8-1054
Rockville, MD 20857
(240) 276-2000
www.samhsa.gov

An agency of the U.S. Department of Health and Human
Services, the Substance Abuse and Mental Health Services
Administration (SAMHSA) helps develop programs for people
who are at risk to become drug abusers. Young people can find
information on SAMHSA's Safe and Drug-Free Schools
programs.

White House Office of National Drug Control Policy
Drug Policy Information Clearinghouse
PO Box 6000
Rockville, MD 20849-6000
(800) 666-3332
www.whitehousedrugpolicy.gov

The White House Office of National Drug Control Policy was
established to develop a national strategy to combat illegal drug
use. The office acts as a liaison serving the different federal drug
investigation and research agencies and helps provide information
to state and local agencies that fight drug abuse.

For Further Reading

Linda Bayer, *Amphetamines and Other Uppers*. Philadelphia: Chelsea House Publishers, 2000. Provides an overview of methamphetamine, how it affects the brain and body, and where users can find help.

Jay Bridges, *Everything You Need to Know About Having an Addictive Personality*. New York: Rosen Publishing Group, 1998. Defines addiction and offers tips on how to avoid getting hooked on drugs, alcohol, gambling, and junk food. For teens who already face addiction, the book recommends techniques and resources they might find helpful in kicking their habits.

Allan B. Cobb, *Speed and Your Brain: The Incredibly Disgusting Story*. New York: Rosen Publishing, 2000. Concentrates on methamphetamine's effects on brain cells and the neurotransmitter dopamine. Also provides a general overview of the dangers of the drug.

Sean Connolly, *Just the Facts: Amphetamines*. Chicago: Heinemann Library, 2001. Examines such issues as the availability of meth, the status of drug laws in America, the impacts of addiction and what treatments are available for users.

Margaret O. Hyde and John F. Setaro, *Drugs 101: An Overview for Teens*. Brookfield, CT: Twenty-first Century Books, 2003. Covers the abuse of several drugs, including methamphetamine. Provides readers with information on the health effects of drug abuse and summarizes the campaign by police to stamp out the narcotics trade.

Donald Ian Macdonald, *Drugs, Drinking and Adolescents.* Chicago: Year Book Medical Publishers, 1989. Dr. Macdonald, a former White House drug policy advisor, offers an overview of the stages of drug abuse by young people, spanning their experimentation with tobacco, alcohol, and marijuana to their addiction to much harder drugs. Also examines the roles of parents, police, and lawmakers in the war on drugs.

Shelagh Ryan Masline, *Drug Abuse and Teens: A Hot Issue.* Berkeley Heights, NJ: Enslow Publishers, 2000. Examines drug abuse trends among teens and includes accounts of addiction by young people, including the experiences of a sixteen-year-old Arizona girl named Heather addicted to meth. Includes tips on resisting peer pressure and developing self-esteem, plus places to contact for information on addiction.

Martin Torgoff, *Can't Find My Way Home: America in the Great Stoned Age. 1945-2000.* New York: Simon and Schuster, 2004. A comprehensive history of illegal drug use in America, covering the Beat writers of the 1950s, hippies of the 1960s, disco clubs of the 1970s, and other eras and trends in drug use.

Paul A. Winters, editor, *Teen Addiction.* San Diego: Greenhaven Press, 1997. Includes numerous essays on teenagers and drug addiction.

Works Consulted

Books

Miklos Laci, *America's Anguish: Illegal Drugs*. Farmington Hills, MI.: Gale Group, 2004. Comprehensive look at the history of drug abuse in the United States, how the government has responded, and the health risks for people who take drugs.

Solomon H. Snyder, *Drugs and the Brain*. New York: Scientific American Library, 1986. Describes the physiological changes that take place in the brain due to drug abuse.

Periodicals

Matt Bai, "White Storm Warning," *Newsweek*, March 31, 1997.

Tom Gorman, "Witness to Fire Says Men Didn't Try to Save Children," *Los Angeles Times*, December 28, 1998.

Cynthia Hanson, "I Had No Idea My Child Was on Drugs," *Ladies Home Journal*, March 1997.

Guy Hargreaves, "Clandestine Drug Labs," *FBI Law Enforcement Bulletin*, April 2000.

Miriam Hill, "Drug Seduces Many to Reckless Behavior," *Philadelphia Inquirer*, February 15, 2005.

Maryann Jensen, "I Got Hooked on Drugs," *McCall's*, February 1997.

Dirk Johnson, "Policing a Rural Plague," *Newsweek*, March 8, 2004.

Walter Kirn, "Crank," *Time*, June 22, 1998.

Anthony R. Lovett, "Wired in California," *Rolling Stone*, May 5,

1994.

Alfred Lubrano, "Police Try to Get a Jump on Meth," *Philadelphia Inquirer*, February 14, 2005.

Dan McGraw, "The Iowan Connection: Powerful Mexican Drug Cartels Have Hit Rural America," *U.S. News and World Report*, March 2, 1998.

Per Ola and Emily D'Aulaire, "A Dangerous Drug Hits the Heartland," *Reader's Digest*, April 1999.

Pennsylvania Crime Commission, *Organized Crime in Pennsylvania: A Decade of Change*, 1990.

People, "Dying for Crystal," February 16, 2004.

Andrew Ross, "The New Suburban High," *Good Housekeeping*, September 1995.

Paul Solotaroff, "A Plague in the Heartland," *Rolling Stone*, January 23, 2003.

Anastasia Toufexis, "There Is No Safe Speed," *Time*, January 8, 1996.

Peter Wilkerson, "America's Drug: Postcards from Tweakville," *Rolling Stone*, February 19, 1998.

Internet Sources

Laurent Belsie, "'Meth' Makers Stealing Volatile Stuff: Fertilizer," *Christian Science Monitor*, February 10, 1999. http://csmonitor.com/cgi-bin/durableRedirect.pl?/durable/1999/02/10/pls3.htm

Charles Bliss, "Methamphetamine: How Effective Are Current Treatment Programs?" Cornerstone Behaviorial Health, www.cornerstonebh.com/meth4.htm.

Betty Ann Bowser, "Drug Trends," *PBS Newshour* Online Transcript, December 10, 1997. www.pbs.org/newshour/bb/health/july-dec97/meth_12-10.html

Edward M. Brecher, "The Consumers Union Report on Illicit and Licit Drugs," *Consumer Reports Magazine*, 1972. www.druglibrary.org/schaffer/Library/studies/cu/

Jeremy Browning, "I Was in a Bad, Bad Way," *Craig Daily Press*,

May 11, 2004. www.craigdailypress.com/section/darkcrystal/storypr/11980

Carl Burnett Jr., "Meth Lab Found in Millersport," *Lancaster Eagle-Gazette*, February 16, 2005. www.lancastereaglegazette.com/news/stories/20050216/localnews/1995214.html

Scott Burns, White House Office of National Drug Policy, "Fighting Methamphetamine in the Heartland," testimony before the House Committee on Government Reform, February 6, 2004. http://reform.house.gov/UploadedFiles/Burns.pdf

Catharyn Campbell, "Investigators, Pharmacists Support Governor's Anti-Meth Package." WATE-Knoxville, January 31, 2005. www.wate.com/global/story.asp?s=2880682&ClientType

Christina M. Currie, "Breaking the Cycle," *Craig Daily Press*, June 1, 2004. www.craigdailypress.com/section/darkcrystal/storypr/12255

Lynn Freehill, "Drug's Latest Victim: Cupcakes," *Des Moines Register*, February 18, 2005. www.desmoinesregister.com/apps/pbcs.dll/article?AID=/20050218/NEWS02/50218

George Gannon, "Police, Social Workers Say Meth Labs Pose Great Risk to Children," *Charleston Daily Mail*, January 10, 2005. www.dailymail.com/news/News/2005011020/display_story.php?sid=2005011020&f

Roman Gokhman, "Tough Year for Suspect's Family," *Grass Valley Union*, January 6, 2005. www.theunion.com/article/20050106/NEWS/101060061/-1/THEMES02

Ruby Gonzales, "Bill Would Require ID to Buy Cold Medications," *Los Angeles Daily News*, February 13, 2005. www.dailynews.com/Stories/0,1413,200%7E20954%7E2708763,00.html

Janice Gregorson, "Any Can, Any House Is a Risky Unknown," *Rochester Post-Bulletin*, June 25, 2001. www,postbulletin.com/meth/stories/day2/65109.shtml

Karin Grunden, "Public Enemy No. 1," *Terre Haute Tribune-Star*, January 19, 2003. www.tribstar.com/articles/2003/01/19/news/export34033.prt

Karin Grunden, "Nearly Fatal Attraction: Young Mother's Addiction Proves Costly," *Terre Haute Tribune-Star*, January 21,

2003. www.tribstar.com/articles/2003/01/21/news/export 34200.prt

Karin Grunden, "Mother Walks Long, Hard Path to Rehabilitation," *Terre Haute Tribune-Star*, January 23, 2003. www.tribstar.com/articles/2003/01/23/news/export34349.prt

Karin Grunden, "Judge Believes Drug Court Offers Solution," *Terre Haute Tribune-Star*, January 24, 2003. www.tribstar.com/articles/2003/01/24/news/export34406.prt

Karin Grunden, "Education Key to Slowing Epidemic," *Terre Haute Tribune-Star*, January 26, 2003. www.tribstar.com/articles/2003/01/26/news/export34470.prt

Amy Hatten, "Meth Use Growing Among Teens," *Craig Daily Press*, May 18, 2004. www.craigdailypress.com/section/dark-crystal/storypr/12081

Amy Hatten, "Former Addict Counsels Youth," *Craig Daily Press*, May 25, 2004. www.craigdailypress.com/section/dark-crystal/storypr/12171

Christina Jewett, "Meth Labs Spreading to Mexico, California's Rural North," *Sacramento Bee*, October 17, 2004. www.shns.com/shns/g_index2.cfm?action=detail&pk=METH-10-17-04

Karen Karbashewski, "Addict Escapes the Lure of Crystal Meth," *Edmonton Examiner*, August 4, 2004. www.edmontonexaminer.com/pages/newsroom/meth_2.html

Karen Karbashewski, "Crystal Meth Takes Terrible Toll on Mind and Body," *Edmonton Examiner*, August 11, 2004. www.edmontonexaminer.com/pages/newsroom/meth_3.html

Amy Olson, "A Family Struggles with Meth," *Rochester Post-Bulletin*, June 23, 2001. www.postbulletin.com/meth/stories/day1/64945.shtml

Amy Olson, "Prison Was the Best Thing to Happen," *Rochester Post-Bulletin*, June 23, 2001. www.postbulletin.com/meth/stories/day1/64939.shtml

Amy Olson, "Jailers Deal with Violent Prisoners, Contaminated Clothes," *Rochester Post-Bulletin*, June 25, 2001. www.postbulletin.com/meth/stories/day2/65107.shtml

Frank Owen, "No Man Is a Crystal Meth User Unto Himself," *New York Times*, August 29, 2004. www.nytimes.com/2004/08/29/fashion/29METH.html?ei=5090&en=00128fed356e0

Sam Skolnik, "Meth Use Linked to Jump in ID, Mail Thefts," *Seattle Post-Intelligencer*, July 23, 2001. http://seattlepi.nwsource.com/local/32357_fraud23.shtml

Dawn Schuett, "Meth's Toll on Children Still Being Evaluated," *Rochester Post Bulletin*, June 27, 2001. www.postbulletin.com/meth/stories/day4/65414.shtml

Dawn Schuett, "As With Any Drug, Getting Off Meth Can Be a Struggle," *Rochester Post Bulletin*, June 28, 2001. www.postbulletin.com/meth/stories/day5/65551.shtml

Mark Stodghill, "Police Seize Two Pounds of Meth," *Duluth News Tribune*, Jan. 12, 2005. www.duluthsuperior.com/mld/duluthsuperior/news/local/10624808.htm?template=c

St. Paul Pioneer Press, "Increasing Cases of 'Meth Mouth' Burden Prisons' Health-Care Budgets," January 9, 2005. www.duluthsuperior.com/mld/duluthsuperior/news/local/1060319.htm

Linda Thomson, "Driver Sentenced in Killing of 2," *Deseret Morning News*, March 12, 2004. http://deseretnews.com/dn/print/1,1442,59504530,00.html

University of Michigan, *Monitoring the Future*, December 2004. www.monitoringthefuture.org.

U.S. Centers for Disease and Control and Prevention, *Morbidity and Mortality Weekly Report*, June 1, 2001. www.cdc.gov/mmwr/.

U.S. Department of Justice, Office of Justice Programs, *Final Report of the Methamphetamine Interagency Task Force, 1999*. http://www.ojp.usdoj.gov/nij/methintf/b.html.

U.S. Department of Justice, Bureau of Justice Statistics, *Drugs and Crime Facts, 2004*. www.ojp.usdoj.gov/bjs/.

U.S. Drug Enforcement Administration, *Drug Trafficking in the United States, 2001*. www.usdoj.gov/dea/concern/drug_trafficking.html.

U.S. Drug Enforcement Administration, "DEA Eliminates Major Source of U.S. Meth," September 23, 2004. www.usdoj.gov

/dea/pubs/pressrel/pr092304.html.

U.S. National Highway Traffic Administration, *Drug and Human Performance Fact Sheets*, March 2004. www.nhtsa. dot.gov/people/injury/research/job185drugs/methamphet-amine.htm.

U.S. National Institute on Drug Abuse, *Methamphetamine Abuse: Epidemiologic Issues and Implications* (Research Monograph 115), 1991. www.nida.nih.gov/pdf/monographs/down-load115.html.

U.S. Substance Abuse and Mental Health Services Administration, *Communication Strategy Guide: A Look at Methampheta-mine Use Among Three Populations, 2000*. http://media. shs.net/prevline/pdfs/index.pdf.

U.S. Substance Abuse and Mental Health Services Administration, *Treatment Episode Data Set Highlights, 2002*. wwwdasis.samhsa.gov/teds02/2002_teds_highlights.pdf.

John Weiss, "A Walk in the Woods Becomes Dangerous," *Rochester Post-Bulletin*, June 26, 2001. www.postbulletin.com /meth/enviro.shtml.

John Weiss, "Used To Be Dead Animals; Now It's Meth Waste," *Rochester Post-Bulletin*, June 26, 2001. www.postbulletin.com /meth/stories/day3/65290.shtml.

Ashley Wiehle, "Local Addict Describes Meth Rehab as 'Roller Coaster Ride,'" *Centralia Morning Sentinel*, June 23, 2004. www.morningsentinel.com.

Ashley Wiehle, "Meth Rehab Centers Provide Round-the-Clock Treatment," *Centralia Morning Sentinel*, June 22, 2004. www.morningsentinel.com.

Ashley Wiehle, "Relapse Not Uncommon on Road to Meth Re-covery," *Centralia Morning Sentinel*, June 20, 2004. www.morningsentinel.com.

White House Office of National Drug Policy, *Pulse Check: Na-tional Trends in Drug Abuse, January 2004*. www.whitehouse-drugpolicy.gov/publications/drugfact/pulsechk/january04/.

Index

Picture Credits

About the Author

Hal Marcovitz is a journalist who lives in Chalfont, Pennsylvania, with his wife, Gail, and daughters Michelle and Ashley. He has written more than sixty books for young readers as well as the satirical novel *Painting the White House*.